MW00624377

FLYING
SAUCERS
FROM THE
KREMLIN

Published by Lisa Hagan Books 2019

www.lisahaganbooks.com

Powered by

SHADOW TEAMS

Copyright © Nick Redfern 2019

ISBN: 978-1-945962-18-9

All Rights Reserved. No part of this publication may be reproduced, stored in a retrieval system, or transmitted in any form, or by any means, electronic, mechanical, photocopying, recording or otherwise without the prior permission in writing of the copyright holders, nor be otherwise circulated in any form or binding or cover other than in which it is published and without a similar condition being imposed on the subsequent publisher.

Cover design and interior layout by Simon Hartshorne

UFOs, Russian Meddling,
Soviet Spies & Cold War Secrets

FLYING SAUCERS FROM THE KREMLIN

NICK REDFERN

CONTENTS

INTRODUCTION

Russian meddling: they are two words that just about everyone has come to know very well in the last few years. Only a fool – or someone with an agenda of a sinister kind – would deny that such meddling occurred. And on a large scale. It clearly did. The outrageous, almost flagrant, ways in which the Russians unfortunately succeeded in manipulating the United States' political arena in 2016 are out there for one and all to see. Without the hacking, without the Russians' widespread use of social media to influence the mindset of the American public, and without the shameful "no evidence of meddling" assertions of certain factions of the right-wing media, the United States would be in a far better shape than it is right now. And, there's little doubt that the Russians were practically in a state of glee when President Donald Trump chose not to take any significant action against the Russians for their intrusive activities. As *CNN* noted on July 16, 2018:

> "U.S. President Donald Trump, in a stunning rebuke of the U.S. intelligence community, declined on Monday to endorse the U.S. government's assessment that Russia interfered in the 2016 presidential election, saying he doesn't 'see any reason why' Russia would be responsible. Instead, Trump - standing alongside Russian President Vladimir Putin - touted Putin's vigorous denial and pivoted to complaining about the Democratic National Committee's server and missing emails from Hillary Clinton's personal account."

Still on the matter of Putin, let's not forget that from 1975 to 1991 he was employed as a foreign intelligence officer in the KGB. *History.com* states, "The KGB was the primary security agency for the Soviet Union from 1954 until its collapse in 1991. The KGB served a multi-faceted role outside of and within the Soviet Union, working as both an intelligence agency and a force of 'secret police.' It was also tasked with some of the same functions as the Department of Homeland Security in the United States today, safeguarding the country from domestic and foreign threats."

What all of this tells us is that the Russian government is not our friend, it's not our buddy. It's a threat to our nation – and to the West as a whole. Short of a nuclear war (which neither side could ever possibly win), the Russians have done whatever they could to try and ensure military superiority over the United States and its allies. There is, however, nothing new about all of this. For decades – and particularly so when the Cold War was at its height – the Russians have sought to find more and more ways to erode our way of life. In the latter part of the 1940s, the Soviet Union embarked on a program designed to use the UFO phenomenon as a dangerous weapon. Not by attacking us with real flying saucers. But, by using the lore, the legend, and the belief-systems that surround the UFO subject. And, in the process, hoping to provoke hysteria and paranoia in the western world.

It's vital to note that *Flying Saucers from the Kremlin* is not a skeptical look at the UFO mystery. Just because, for years, the Russians planted and circulated numerous bogus stories of UFOs, doesn't mean there isn't a real mystery to be solved. As I personally see it, there certainly *is* a genuine puzzle to figure out. It remains steadfastly unresolved. It's important that I make that distinction: there *are* real UFOs and there *are* deliberately-crafted lies *concerning* UFOs. Maybe, the saucers are the products of government agencies. They could be the creations of extraterrestrials.

Possibly of interdimensional creatures. Or, the work of something even stranger (time-travelers, maybe?). There could be multiple origins, rather than just one. That's an issue that we can ponder on forever and a day. But, trying to figure out what UFOs *are*, is not the goal of this book. I'm here to demonstrate to you how a real strange presence in our midst became entangled in the Cold War between the West and the Soviet Union.

Come with me now as we go on a wild and controversial ride into both the past and the present. You'll see how the Russians tried to use the Contactee movement of the 1950s to their distinct advantage; spread tales of crashed UFOs and alien autopsies; recruited American UFO enthusiasts – who also had connections to the U.S. government - into their strange games; created bogus "government documents" (including at least some of the much-debated Majestic 12 papers); forged links with saucer-seekers in both the U.K. and Australia; and even incorporated the history of the AIDS virus into their disturbing agenda. And there's much much more.

No such thing as Russian meddling? Don't make me laugh.

1.

"THE MORE I OBSERVED THESE OBJECTS THE MORE UPSET I BECAME"

Before we get to the matter of how and why the U.S. Government was so concerned about a Russian-UFO connection, it's important to understand the fraught climate that existed in the United States in the post-Second World War era and beyond. And, also how it allowed for UFO-themed shenanigans of a truly weird form to nurture and soon expand –into the 1950s and onward. We're talking about the "Reds under the beds" scares that had a decisive grip on elements of the populace. In many ways, they were driven by one man: Wisconsin Republican Senator Joseph McCarthy. He, more than anyone else, seeded in the minds of many the notion that there were Soviets, and Russian sympathizers, here, there and just about everywhere in the United States. For the best part of a half a decade, McCarthy hammered home what he saw as a dangerous communist plot to undermine the United States and to destroy the fabric of American society. In McCarthy's mind, *they* were everywhere. Americans needed to know that. Time was running out for the land of the free, as McCarthy saw it.

It's very easy to understand how and why such fears of the Russians began to surface – and quickly too. There was widespread relief when the Allies won the Second World War in 1945. But, then, not long after Hitler and his cronies were thankfully gone, the world was faced with yet another potential enemy, one that was just as dangerous to national security as the Germans: the

Soviet Union. Four years after the Japanese cities of Nagasaki and Hiroshima were turned into rubble and ash, and their citizens were killed in six-figures, the Russians well and truly flexed their muscles by detonating *their* very own atomic bomb. The world collectively shuddered. Fears of a looming, civilization-ending, Third World War understandably grew.

It was also during this state of flux and fear that the House Un-American Committee (HUAC) – which was created in 1938 - was busily trying to dig out Soviet agents and U.S. citizens who had pro-Russian beliefs. The sponsor and first chairman of the HUAC was Martin Dies, Jr., a Democratic member of the United States House of Representatives. As we'll soon see, in a strange way, Dies, Jr. had a tie to one of the key players in the early years of Ufology. That same player was suspected of being a communist, as we'll also soon see.

The Freedom of Information Act has shown that the FBI, working with the HUAC, targeted movie-stars, writers, poets, musicians, and just about anyone who seemed to be anything less than a full-on, patriotic American. Often, the accusations were completely bogus. One year after Russia showed the world that it, too, now had the bomb, Congress initiated the McCarran Internal Security Act. It allowed the government to keep a careful and even closer watch on anyone in the United States who might be considered not exactly one hundred percent kosher.

Famously – or, maybe, infamously would be far more correct – in February 1950, McCarthy spoke at the Ohio County Women's Republican Club. In a raging bull style, he claimed that hundreds of communists were actively working within the U.S. Department of State. The claim became big news, despite the fact that McCarthy wouldn't – or possibly *couldn't* – provide the goods to support his eye-opening claims. Nevertheless, the tidal wave of unsupported statements continued to make big, nationwide news. Three years on, McCarthy was put in control of the Committee on Government Operations. Still a senator, McCarthy now had even more power to root out what he saw as a vast number of closet-communists. He even maintained that the U.S. military had been infiltrated, too – and to a major degree. It was, however, when McCarthy's hearings were broadcast on television that entire swathes of the population saw McCarthy as someone seemingly attacking those he had in his sights, but without much in the way of evidence.

The whole thing left a very bad taste in the mouths of many, to the extent that nearly all of McCarthy's supporters finally walked away from him, effectively leaving him weakened and, finally, ineffective. But, the memories of McCarthyism proved to be both powerful and enduring, to the extent that even with McCarthy largely gone, there were fears that Russia was *still* working hard, and secretly, to destroy the fabric of American society. From the summer of 1947, those same concerns related to all-things of a flying saucer nature.

It should be noted that the Russians' UFO program was far from being the only strange operation designed to create fear in the United States. As the Freedom of Information Act has shown, in 1951 the FBI – to its grave concern – heard fear-inducing rumors that the Soviets had secretly managed to smuggle an atomic bomb into the United States. Worse still, the Bureau's source – an unknown figure in Brazil – claimed that the bomb was primed and ready to go. Right in the heart of New York City. Hundreds of thousands could be dead in seconds, vaporized; maybe even *millions*. FBI special-agents spent several years chasing down just about every lead possible. Eventually, however, they gave up the chase, suspecting strongly that the whole story was a fabrication, one that was specifically designed to ignite terror. For a while, it did exactly that. Moving on, in 1952 the Soviets had their agents spread bogus tales claiming that the United States' cattle-herd had been infected with a deadly virus. It wasn't true. But, it, too, reached the eyes and the ears of the FBI. As with the story of the smuggled atomic device, this tale also had certain agencies in a state of consternation, but, eventually, it too fizzled out. I mention this to show that all manner of strange operations were afoot in that early Cold War era, and their creators were all intent on causing mayhem in the minds of the U.S. government, intelligence agencies, and the military.

The UFO program, though, was surely the strangest of them all.

There's absolutely no doubt that had pilot Kenneth Arnold not encountered a veritable squadron of strange-looking aircraft near Mt. Rainier, Washington State on the afternoon of June 24, 1947, there would never have been an opportunity for the Russians – and for the United States, too, as we'll soon see – to exploit a very real phenomenon of mystifying origins and nature for psychological and military gain. But, as history has shown, Arnold most assuredly *did* have that now-legendary encounter. Whether Arnold encountered a number of extraterrestrial craft, advanced creations of the Soviet Union, or the then-latest developments of the U.S. military, remains unknown. The theories are many. Hard answers are scant. Let's take a look at what happened to Arnold on that particular day which changed the world. Arnold said...

The following story of what I observed over the Cascade Mountains, as impossible as it may seem, is positively true. I never asked nor wanted any notoriety for just accidentally being in the right spot at the right time to observe what I did. I reported something that I know any pilot would have reported. I don't think that in any way my observation was due to any sensitivity of eye-sight or judgment than what is considered normal for any pilot. On June 24th, Tuesday, 1947, I had finished my work for the Central Air Service at Chehalis, Washington, and at about two o'clock I took off from Chehalis, Washington, airport with the intention of going to Yakima, Washington. My trip was delayed for an hour to search for a large marine transport that supposedly went down near or around the southwest side of Mt. Rainier in the state of Washington and to date has never been found.

I flew directly toward Mt. Rainier after reaching an altitude of about 9,500 feet, which is the approximate elevation of the high plateau from which Mt. Rainier rises. I had made one sweep of this high plateau to the westward, searching all of the various ridges for this marine ship and flew to the west down and near the ridge side of the canyon where Ashford, Washington, is located. Unable to see anything that looked like the lost ship, I made a 360 degree turn to the right and above the little city of Mineral, starting again toward Mt. Rainier. I climbed back up to an altitude of approximately 9,200 feet. The air was so smooth that day that it was a real pleasure flying and, as most pilots do when the air is smooth and they are flying at a higher altitude, I trimmed out my airplane in the direction of Yakima, Washington, which was almost directly east of my position and simply sat in my plane observing the sky and the terrain.

There was a DC-4 to the left and to the rear of me approximately fifteen miles distance, and I should judge, at 14,000 foot elevation. The sky and air was clear as crystal. I hadn't flown more than two or three minutes on my course when a bright flash reflected on my airplane.

It startled me as I thought I was too close to some other aircraft. I looked every place in the sky and couldn't find where the reflection had come from until I looked to the left and the north of Mt. Rainier where I observed a chain of nine peculiar looking aircraft flying from north to south at approximately 9,500 foot elevation and going, seemingly, in a definite direction of about 170 degrees.

They were approaching Mt. Rainier very rapidly, and I merely assumed they were jet planes. Anyhow, I discovered that this was where the reflection had come from, as two or three of them every few seconds would dip or change their course slightly, just enough for the sun to strike them at an angle that reflected brightly on my plane. These objects being quite far away, I was unable for a few seconds to make out their shape or their formation. Very shortly they approached Mt. Rainier, and I observed their outline against the snow quite plainly.

I thought it was very peculiar that I couldn't find their tails but assumed they were some type of jet plane. I was determined to clock their speed, as I had two definite points I could clock them by; the air was so clear that it was very easy to see objects and determine their approximate shape and size at almost fifty miles that day. I remember distinctly that my sweep second hand on my eight day clock, which is located on my instrument panel, read one minute to 3 P.M. as the first object of this formation passed the southern edge of Mt. Rainier. I watched these objects with great interest as I had never before observed airplanes flying so close to the mountain tops, flying directly south to southeast down the hog's back of a mountain range. I would estimate their elevation could have varied a thousand feet one way or another up or down, but they were pretty much on the horizon to me which would indicate they were near the same elevation as I was.

They flew like the many times I have observed geese [sic] to fly in a rather diagonal chain-like line as if they were linked together. They seemed to hold a definite direction but rather swerved in and out of the high mountain peaks. Their speed at the time did not impress me particularly, because I knew that our army and air forces had planes that went very fast. What kept bothering me as I watched them flip and flash in the sun right along their path was the fact that I couldn't make out any tail on them, and I am sure that any pilot would justify more than a second look at such a plane. I observed them quite plainly, and I estimate my distance from them, which was almost at right angles, to be between twenty to twenty-five miles. I knew they must be very large to observe their shape at that distance, even on as clear a day as it was that Tuesday, In fact I compared a zeus [sic: it should be "Dzus"] fastener or cowling tool I had in my pocket with them - holding it up on them and holding it up on the DC-4 - that I could observe at quite a distance to my left, and they seemed smaller than the DC-4; but, I should judge their span would have been as wide as the furtherest [sic] engines on each side of the fuselage of the DC-4.

The more I observed these objects the more upset I became, as I am accustomed and familiar with most all objects flying whether I am close to the ground or at higher altitudes. I observed the chain of these objects passing another high snow-covered ridge in between Mt. Rainier and Mt. Adams and as the first one was passing the south crest of this ridge, the last object was entering the northern crest of the ridge. As I was flying in the direction of this particular ridge, I measured it and found it to be approximately five miles; I could safely assume that the chain of these saucer-like objects were at least five miles long. I could quite accurately determine their pathway due to the fact that there were several high peaks that were a little this side of them as well as higher peaks on the other side of their pathway.

As the last unit of this formation passed the southern-most high snow-covered crest of Mt. Adams, I looked at my sweep second hand and it showed that they had travelled the distance in one minute and forty-two seconds. Even at the time this timing did not upset me as I felt confident after I would land there would be some explanation of what I saw. A number of newsmen and experts suggested that I might have been seeing reflections or even a mirage. This I know to be absolutely false, as I observed these objects not only through the glass of my airplane but turned my airplane sideways where I could open my window and observe them with a completely unobstructed view. (Without sunglasses.) Even though two minutes seems like a very short time to one on the ground, in the air in two minutes time a pilot can observe a great many things and anything within his sight of vision probably as many as fifty or sixty times.

I continued my search for the marine plane for another fifteen or twenty minutes and while searching, what I had just observed kept going through my mind. I became more disturbed, so after taking a last look at Tieton Reservoir, I headed for Yakima. I might add that my complete observation of these objects, which I could even follow by their flashes as they passed Mt. Adams, was around two and one-half or three minutes -- although, by the time they reached Mt. Adams they were out of my range of vision as far as determining shape or form. Of course, when the sun reflected from one or two or three of these units, they appeared to be completely round; but, I am making a drawing to the best of my ability, which I am including, as to the shape I observed these objects to be as they passed the snow covered ridges as well as Mt. Rainier. When these objects were flying approximately straight and level, they were just a black thin line and when they flipped was the only time I could get a judgment as to their size.

These objects were holding an almost constant elevation; they did not seem to be going up or coming down, such as would be the case of rockets or artillery shells. I am convinced in my own mind that they were some type of airplane, even though they didn't conform with the many aspects of the conventional type of planes that I know.

Although these objects have been reported by many other observers throughout the United States, there have been six or seven other accounts written by some of these observers that I can truthfully say must have observed the same thing that I did; particularly, the descriptions of the three Western [Cedar City, Utah] Air Lines employees, the gentleman [pilot] from Oklahoma City and the locomotive engineer from Illinois, plus Capt. Smith and Co-Pilot Stevens of United Air Lines.

Some descriptions could not be very accurate taken from the ground unless these saucer-like disks were at a great height and there is a possibility that all of the people who observed peculiar objects could have seen the same thing I did, but, it would have been very difficult from the ground to observe these for more than four or five seconds, and there is always the possibility of atmospheric moisture and dust near the ground which could distort one's vision.

I have in my possession letters from all over the Unites States and people who profess that these objects have been observed over other portions of the world, principally Sweden, Bermuda, and California. I would have given almost anything that day to have had a movie camera with a telephoto lens and from now on I will never be without one - - but, to continue further with my story. When I landed at Yakima airport I described what I had seen to my very good friend, Al Baxter, who listened patiently and was very courteous but in a joking way didn't believe me. I did not accurately measure the distance between these two mountains until I landed at Pendleton, Oregon, that same day where I told a number of pilot friends of mine what I had observed and they did not scoff or laugh but suggested they might be guided missiles or something new. In fact several former Army pilots informed me that they had been briefed before going into combat overseas that they might see objects of similar shape and design as I described and assured me that I wasn't dreaming or going crazy.

I quote Sonny Robinson, a former Army Air Forces pilot who is now operating dusting operations at Pendleton, Oregon, "that what you observed, I am convinced, is some type of jet or rocket propelled ship that is in the process of being tested by our government or even it could possibly be by some foreign government." Anyhow, the news that I had observed these spread very rapidly and before the night was over I was receiving telephone calls from all parts of the world; and, to date, I have not received one telephone call or one letter of scoffing or disbelief. The only disbelief that I know of was what was printed in the papers.

I look at this whole ordeal as not something funny as some people have made it out to be. To me it is mighty serious and since I evidently did observe something that at least Mr. John Doe on the street corner or Pete Andrews on the ranch has never heard about, is no reason that it does not exist. Even though I openly invited an investigation by the Army and the FBI as to the authenticity of my story or a mental or a physical examination as to my capabilities, I have received no interest from these two important protective forces of our country; I will go so far as to assume that any report I gave to the United and Associated Press and over the radio on two different occasions which apparently set the nation buzzing, if our Military intelligence was not aware of what I observed, they would be the very first people that I could expect as visitors.

I have received lots of requests from people who told me to make a lot of wild guesses. I have based what I have written here in this article on positive facts and as far as guessing what it was I observed, it is just as much a mystery to me as it is to the rest of the world.

In no time at all, the U.S. military and the FBI swung into action. Answers were needed. Not many came. But the Russians did, in a strange and unforeseen way.

2.

"THE ACHIEVEMENT OF NATIONAL OBJECTIVES"

As well as investigating what appeared to be legitimate, mystifying UFO encounters in the summer of 1947, the FBI also studied the possibility that the Russians were recruiting communists within the United States to provoke fear – and were using aspects of the UFO enigma to heighten that fear. Barely a month after the Kenneth Arnold situation erupted and caused worldwide amazement, FBI Special Agent S.W. Reynolds had a face-to-face chat with Brigadier George F. Schulgen, of the Intelligence Branch of the Army Air Corps Intelligence. The reason was, in part, to address that controversial matter of potential Russian manipulation of the UFO issue. In fact, it was this theory – rather than matters relative to aliens or to highly classified U.S. military programs – that was at the forefront of Brigadier Schulgen's thinking. FBI records show Schulgen informed Reynolds that "*the first reported sightings might have been by individuals of Communist sympathies with the view to causing hysteria and fear of a secret weapon* [italics mine]." Schulgen's team suspected that many flying saucer sightings were not what they seemed to be. Rather, they were completely fabricated tales – with no real UFO component attached to them at all, but driven by a Soviet operation to maximize deep concern in the United States. The Russian program had begun.

On August 14, 1947, the FBI got word – via newspaper articles contained in "the Los Angeles papers" of the day – that, to quote the FBI, "Soviet espionage agents had been instructed to determine the facts relative to the flying discs. The article carried a Washington date-line and indicated that Red espionage agents had been ordered to solve the question of flying discs, the Russians being of the opinion that this might be some new form of defense perfected by the American military." It should also be noted, however, that the FBI was worried that those same Russian agents cited in the L.A. press were actually in the United States for other reasons. Namely, to determine how effectively they - the Soviets - were disrupting the U.S. by conjuring up bogus tales of unidentified flying objects. When questioned by the media on this matter, the FBI stated that it had no information relative to such a story. Uh-huh.

FBI Special Agent D.M. Ladd, of the Bureau's Domestic Intelligence Division, said that "in the event any inquiries were made concerning such a story, that the story should be flatly denied in so far as the FBI was concerned." Nevertheless, behind closed doors elements of the FBI were still speculating on the astounding theory that many UFO reports were complete fabrications; fanciful tales put together at the behest of influential and powerful figures in the Moscow Kremlin - to give it its full name – which is the official residence of the President of the Russian Federation.

While addressing the same timeframe - the latter part of the 1940s - we see evidence that the U.S. Government chose to follow the lead of the Soviets when it came to the matter of manipulating the UFO controversy. That's to say, U.S. Intelligence realized that if the Soviets could theoretically use bogus UFO tales as a means to try and keep the American people in a state of concern, then why couldn't Uncle Sam do exactly the same – but with *their* operations aimed at the citizens of the likes of Moscow and Saint Petersburg?

Evidence that the U.S. intelligence community entered into the very same realm of mind-games that the Russians initiated, can be found in the pages of a *Project Grudge* "Technical Report" on UFOs; *Grudge* being one of the early UFO projects of the U.S. military. The report was prepared by the U.S. Air Force in August 1949. The writer of the lengthy *Project Grudge* document states in part the following: "Upon eliminating several additional incidents due to vagueness and duplication, there remain 228 incidents, which are considered in this report. Thirty of these could not be explained, because there was found to be insufficient evidence on which to base a conclusion."

It's the following words, however, that really stand out. The military made a recommendation that "[the] *Psychological Warfare Division and other governmental agencies interested in psychological warfare be informed of the results of this study* [italics mine]." Quite possibly, it was this document - more than any other of that particular era - that led the U.S. Government to initiate a highly secret program to manipulate the flying saucer phenomenon and mess with the minds of Soviet Premier, Joseph Stalin, and his goons. Take a look at how the Pentagon defines psychological warfare. It is, in the military's own words, "*The planned use of propaganda and other psychological actions having the primary purpose of influencing the opinions, emotions, attitudes, and behavior of hostile foreign groups in such a way as to support the achievement of national objectives* [italics mine]."

This demonstrates that the earliest U.S. military-controlled UFO research programs weren't just about investigating sightings of strange things in the sky. The operations were also focused on creating utterly bogus flying saucer-themed stories; amazing yarns born out of psychological warfare operations and ingenious propaganda. The Russians were doing it to our people, and we were doing likewise to theirs. What a strange and twisted game it all became.

3.

"RUSSIAN WRITING" AND ROSWELL

If the words of a man named Alfred O'Donnell are to be trusted (and, admittedly, it's a *very* big *if*), then the Russians were behind the biggest and most well-known UFO case of all: Roswell. We'll come back to O'Donnell and his controversy-filled claims shortly. There's absolutely no doubt whatsoever that something very strange occurred on the huge, sprawling Foster Ranch in Lincoln County, New Mexico in the first week of July 1947. On the day in question – the precise date of which is still not entirely clear – ranch foreman William Ware "Mack" Brazel came across a huge field of silvery debris on that very same ranch. It stretched across an area of around six hundred feet. Brazel's sheep made it very clear to him that they had no intention of trying to make their way through the mass of foil-like material. Clearly, something had plummeted from the skies on the night before. But what was it?

With all the talk of flying saucers that had been going on for the past two weeks or so, it was practically inevitable that Brazel and his neighbors would ponder on the amazing possibility that just such a craft had come down. Right in their very neighborhood. Brazel contacted the local police, who then put in a call to the relatively nearby Roswell Army Air Field. It wasn't long before the military descended on the ranch, setting up road-blocks, and warning people to keep away from the ranch. There were chilling rumors of death-threats made to those who dared to speak out about what they had seen, of the discovery of small, decomposing humanoid bodies strewn about a rugged second site, and of a semi-intact vehicle discovered at a nearby third site.

Incredibly, the base's public information officer, Walter Haut, put out a press release stating that a "flying disc" had been recovered. He had the full permission of the higher-ups to circulate that very same press release. Other media outlets referred to a "flying saucer." Did a UFO slam into the ground on the huge ranch? Was a huge cover-up put into place to hide the incredible truth? That very much depends on who you care to ask. One day after the Haut release caused so much amazement, personnel at the Roswell Army Air Field claimed that the whole thing was nothing but a big mistake; a most embarrassing one, some might say. What had *really* come down, the military was now insisting, was a weather-balloon. And that was all. There wasn't even a word about bodies. It would be decades before the military would tackle the thorny body controversy. This was far from being the end of the story, though. The mystery was resurrected in the mid-1970s by researchers Bill Moore and Stanton Friedman. In 1980, Moore's book, *The Roswell Incident* – co-written with Charles Berlitz - was published and added more to the story. Tom Carey, Kevin Randle and Don Schmitt added further to the case, writing their own books on the still-mystifying event. By the 1990s, just about everyone had heard of Roswell.

In early 1993, the then-Congressman for New Mexico, Steven Schiff, began to take an interest in the Roswell controversy. His attempts to get to the heart of the mystery, which involved approaching both the U.S. Air Force and the National Archives for answers, failed. Completely. Time and again he was stonewalled. Schiff quickly realized he was being given a definitive runaround. He was far from happy and was not the kind of person to cross swords with. After initially *asking* for answers, Schiff soon *demanded* them. Schiff approached the Government Accountability Office (at the time, it was called the General Accounting Office), and requested that they look into the matter. The GAO was up for the challenge. Was the truth of what happened all those years earlier on the Foster Ranch about to surface?

When the Pentagon learned of Schiff's attempts to get the GAO to uncover the facts surrounding Roswell, U.S. Air Force staff hastily began working on their *own* investigations into the case. They also came quickly to an answer. As the GAO noted in 1994: "The Air Force report concluded that there was no dispute that something happened near Roswell in July 1947 and that all available official material indicated the most likely source of the wreckage recovered was one of the project MOGUL balloon trains. At the time of the Roswell crash, project MOGUL was a highly classified U.S. effort to determine the state of Soviet nuclear weapons research using balloons that carried radar reflectors."

It's very important, however, to note that all of this was simply the Air Force's opinion. In fact, not even a single, solitary, military document has ever surfaced showing that a Mogul balloon was recovered at the crash site. The Air Force's opinion was exactly that: an opinion. It should be noted, too, that no documented evidence has ever been found supporting the weather-balloon and flying saucer theories, either. And, what of the claims of strange bodies having been found on the ranch? Back in 1994, the Air Force dismissed all the claims that bodies of any kind - animals, aliens or people – were found. The Air Force's reasoning was to the point: Mogul balloons didn't carry crews, so, how could any bodies be found? Three years later, in 1997 – which was Roswell's 50th anniversary – the Air Force reversed its stance and said that bodies, of a sort, *were* found, after all. But, they were crash-test dummies used in high-altitude, parachute-based programs. When the mainstream press quickly discovered that the "dummy pro-gram" didn't actually begin until the early 1950s, and were not up and running in 1947, the Air Force seethed and squirmed. No wonder that the Roswell case continues to provoke such interest. The incident hit the media big-time yet again; this time it was in 2011. It was as a result of the research and probing of an investigative journalist named Annie Jacobsen.

Over the years, Annie Jacobsen has written a number of books on the matter of government secrecy. They include *Surprise, Kill, Vanish*; *The Pentagon's Brain*; *Phenomena*; *Operation Paperclip*; and *Area 51*. It's the latter title that we need to focus our attentions on. Jacobsen's *Area 51* is a solid, insightful and illuminating study of the history and secret world of Nevada's infamous, impenetrable base. When *Area 51* was published, what really caught the attention of both the UFO research community and the nation's media was the testimony that Jacobsen had received on Roswell. It all came from a solitary whistleblower. In the pages of her book, Jacobsen's source for the Roswell story is not identified (although he *does* appear, by his real name, in *other* sections of the book that specifically *don't* deal with Roswell). We know, though, thanks to the digging of UFO researcher Tony Bragalia that the man in question was one Alfred O'Donnell, who died on April 9, 2015, then in his nineties. He was described as "one of the elite engineers from EG&G." And why might EG&G be? As Bragalia noted:

> "Founded as Edgerton, Germeshausen and Grier (EG&G) the company was acquired by URS Corporation some years ago. URS employs over 50,000 and is the leading designer and builder of federal classified facilities in the United States. They work with military as well as with

the Intelligence Community (particularly the NSA) in constructing and operating some of our nation's most sensitive and secret facilities."

Now, let's take a look at what O'Donnell claimed was the dark truth behind the Roswell legend.

According to data that Alfred O'Donnell claimed he was exposed to during his time working for EG&G, what came down outside of Roswell, New Mexico in July 1947 was not a UFO. Nor was it a weather-balloon or a Mogul balloon. And there was, apparently, not even a single crash-test dummy anywhere in sight. O'Donnell made the controversial and sensational claim that the craft and its crew originated in the Soviet Union. But, we're not talking about your average aircraft. The same goes for those aboard it, too. O'Donnell said that Joseph Stalin – the General Secretary of the Communist Party of the Soviet Union from 1922 to 1952 and Premier from 1941 to 1953 – was the driving force behind what was, allegedly, a diabolical, manipulative plot designed to make the U.S. Government and the people of the United States think that an alien invasion was underway. The purpose: to plunge America into a state of overwhelming terror.

It's worth my time mentioning that in early 2006 I was given an almost identical story from a former employee of Area 51 (where Alfred O'Donnell spent some time). The scenario was practically the same: physically altered people were flown – from Russia to the United States - aboard a strange-looking aircraft, as a means to try and convince the United States government that the nation was about to be invaded by extraterrestrials. The story, as it was told to me, was first published in my 2010 book, *The NASA Conspiracies*, one year before Jacobsen's book appeared. This suggests that O'Donnell was not the only one with Area 51 connections who had been exposed to this strange believe-it-or-not type tale.

O'Donnell said that Stalin had secretly enlisted into the plot Dr. Josef Mengele, one of the vilest and most deranged and dangerous figures of the 20th century. Mengele spent a great deal of his time at Auschwitz, a complex comprised of more than forty camps in then-occupied Poland, at which where more than one million people died in horrible fashions at the hands of Nazi scum. Mengele had a very disturbing fascination with dwarfs, to the extent that he undertook awful experiments on them. As Annie Jacobsen states, Mengele "removed parts of children's craniums and replaced them with bones from larger, adult skulls." He also removed the eyes from children who exhibited various forms of dwarfism. Some of the experiments led the children to lose all of their hair. By this point, you might have deduced where things are leading. Stalin had a warped plan to have a number of child-dwarfs physically altered by Mengele and his team of doctors (although, calling them "doctors" is a disservice to doctors all around the world). They would go from looking like children to resembling something unearthly. Then, there was the matter of the "alien spaceship" that Stalin needed to complete the ruse.

So O'Donnell's tale goes, Stalin brought in a team of experts in the field of aviation and had them create two strange-looking aircraft based upon the near-unique designs of a pair of aircraft engineers. They were Walter and Reimar Horten, both born in Germany; Walter in 1913 and Reimar in 1915. There is no doubt that during the Second World War the pair constructed some very strange aerial vehicles. According to what Annie Jacobsen was told, by 1947 Stalin's infernal plan was just about ready to go. An obvious question needs answering: how on Earth could a number of poor, surgically-altered children fly a highly advanced aircraft from Russia to the United States? Well, according to Alfred O'Donnell, they didn't. He claimed that the vehicle in which the children were strapped in was remotely-controlled by the crew of the second Horten-type craft.

The plot was for the aircraft containing the children to land in a visible location in the United States and then have the children exit the strange-looking craft and present themselves to the highest echelons of the U.S. Government. The outcome: a unanimous belief that an alien invasion was about to begin, and widespread chaos and fear across the land would inevitably follow. It didn't quite work out like that, though. As history has shown, the craft crashed rather than landed, and all of the action went down on the Foster Ranch, New Mexico; not on the lawns of the White House, as, perhaps, may have been the plan. So, with just (a) a few locals in Lincoln County, (b) various personnel from the Roswell Army Air Field, and (c) a group of senior military personnel in the Pentagon, in the know, the Army Air Force quickly shut everything down and put a plan into process that revolved around nothing more threatening than a weather-balloon. The same team then put the fear of God into the likes of Mack Brazel – ensuring that he would never talk; which, history has shown, after 1947 he did not. And they retrieved the smashed craft and the badly damaged bodies of the children, along with two survivors of the flight. Everything was then swiftly flown to what is now Wright-Patterson Air Force Base, Dayton, Ohio; the home of the Foreign Technology Division. In 1951, all of the recovered evidence was secretly transported to Area 51, Nevada, where they are still said to be held to this day. That, basically, is the claim of Alfred O'Donnell. It's well-thought out, but it most definitely has its flaws.

It is a fact that the Horten brothers *did* work on aircraft that were radical in design and appearance. There's a December 1947 document that focuses on what the U.S. military knew, at that time, on matters relative to the Horten brother and flying saucers. It's a document that was written by a Lieutenant Colonel Harry H. Pretty for the H.Q. Berlin Command, Office of Military Government for Germany (U.S.). Titled *Horten Brothers (Flying Saucers)*, it was sent to the Deputy Director of Intelligence, European Command, Frankfurt, Germany, U.S. Army for study. Lieutenant Colonel Pretty's report shows that although the Horten brothers had certainly worked on some revolutionary designs, *none* could be said to be definitive flying saucers.

A U.S. Air Force document of January 3, 1952 (on the subject of UFO sightings investigated by the Air Force in the late 1940s and early 1950s) from Brigadier General W.M. Garland to General John A. Samford, Air Force Director of Intelligence is highly intriguing, as it touches upon the work of the Horten brothers, Walter and Reimar. It starts: "It is logical to relate the reported sightings to the known development of aircraft, jet propulsion, rockets and range extension capabilities in Germany and the USSR. In this connection, it is to be noted that certain developments by the Germans, particularly the Horten wing, jet propulsion, and refueling, combined with their extensive employment of V-l and V-2 weapons during World War II, lend credence to the possibility that the flying objects may be of German and Russian origin."

The document continues: "The developments mentioned above were completed and operational between 1941 and 1944 *and subsequently fell into the hands of the Soviets at the end of the war* [italics mine]. There is evidence that the Germans were working on these projects as far back as 1931 to 1938. Therefore it may be assumed that the Germans had at least a 7 to 10 year lead over the United States."

Some might say that this bizarre tale has a degree of plausibility attached to it. For example, it should be noted that both Reimar Horten and Josef Mengele moved to Argentina. Mengele did so in July 1949, later fleeing to Paraguay and then Brazil, while trying to avoid extradition on war-crimes. He died in 1979. Reimar Horten left for Argentina in the post-Second World War era and died there in 1994.

There are, however, significant red-flags that need to be addressed. Alfred O'Donnell told Annie Jacobsen that the interior of the craft that came down on the Foster Ranch in 1947 contained "Russian writing" and "letters from the Cyrillic alphabet." If the Russians wanted the craft to be perceived by the U.S. Government as being extraterrestrial in origin, what would prompt the Russians to adorn it with examples of their very own writing? Such an action would be ridiculous and would quickly reveal to the United States government the Russian craft for what it really was; surely causing the entire "alien invasion" plan to collapse in rapid-time. We should also note that the Roswell affair occurred in early July 1947. The Kenneth Arnold incident occurred only two weeks before. How could the Russians have constructed the two aircraft, surgically altered the "crew," and remotely flown the vehicles to the United States in such a short time-frame after Arnold spoke out? Unless, of course, the Russians were behind Arnold's sighting, too, and the plan to fly the craft which crashed on the ranch was *already* in place and planned months earlier. There's also the issue of that huge debris field, which was said to have covered an area of roughly six hundred feet. With such a huge amount of damage done to the vehicle, one has to wonder how anyone could have survived the crash; never mind two children. It's an unfortunate and grisly fact that in many high-speed, high-altitude air accidents, the bodies of those on-board are pulverized beyond recognition. But, two somehow managed to survive the Roswell crash?

When it comes to the matter of trying to resolve all of this, there are several theories we might want to ponder on: (a) that Alfred O'Donnell was directed by Area 51-based colleagues to feed such a sensational story to Annie Jacobsen, as a means to try and discredit and "contaminate" the legitimate top secret material she had uncovered and published in her 2011 *Area 51* book; (b) that the story was the creation of right-wing extremists who had an agenda designed to instill the very disturbing image of superior, advanced, Nazi technology in our midst; or, (c) that the events broadly occurred as O'Donnell described them: a truly horrific effort by the Soviets to use the UFO phenomenon as a means to try and psychologically destabilize the United States by faking the first wave of an alien invasion.

Now, we'll see an example of how the United States government hit back against the early saucer-based operations of the Soviets.

4.

"SOME SORT OF PSYCHOLOGICAL WARFARE OPERATION"

The strange story of the alleged UFO crash at Aztec, New Mexico in March 1948 – and the recovery of a number of dead "little men" at the site - is a real hotbed of lies, disinformation, and shady characters. Most of those same characters were best avoided by those with dollars to spare. The tale was made infamous in the pages of Frank Scully's 1950 blockbuster, *Behind the Flying Saucers*; it was a book that turned out to be a huge seller. Today, the Aztec affair is seen by some ufologists as Roswell's "little brother;" "skeleton in the cupboard" might be a far more apt description, however. Many researchers of the UFO phenomenon dismiss the Aztec incident as nothing but a hoax; one which was perpetrated by a shady businessman/conman named Silas Newton. His less-than-shining FBI file can be accessed at the FBI's website, *The Vault*. When it came to stories of aliens from faraway worlds, making money was always the goal for Newton. And the *only* goal. Along for the ride with Newton was Leo Gebauer. He was a quasi-scientist and the Igor to Newton's ego-driven Dr. Frankenstein. There is, though, a very interesting and extremely odd aspect to the Newton/Aztec story. It serves to demonstrate how the UFO phenomenon was becoming the tool of manipulative disinformation specialists in the intelligence community. And not just of the Soviet Union. The United States was getting into the strange game, too.

Back in 1998, the late Karl Pflock, ufologist and CIA employee (sometimes at the same time…), was approached by a still-anonymous source who had something very interesting to say about the Aztec caper, and about Newton too. It was a decidedly weird series of revelations that Pflock surely never anticipated receiving. To his dying day, Pflock refused to reveal the name of his informant in the shadows – rumors, however, were that the person may have been a nephew of Silas Newton – but, Pflock did say that all of the lunchtime meetings with his source occurred between July 11 and September 24, 1998 and took place in a restaurant in Bernalillo, New Mexico. As the story goes, Pflock's informant had in their hands twenty-seven pages taken, or rather torn, from an old and faded, lined journal. No prizes for guessing who that journal had belonged to. That's right, sly, old Silas Newton. Pflock was told that Newton had kept journals and diaries not just for years, but for *decades*. They were jammed with entertaining tales of sexual conquests, of Hollywood starlets, of the fleecing of the rich and the gullible, and of wild adventures across the United States. The outcome of all this? Newton decided, around the turn of the 1970s, that it was right about time for him to write-up his version of the Aztec controversy. It would surely have been a definitive page-turner. Death, however, inconveniently intervened in 1972, when Newton passed away in his mid-eighties. What happened to all of those journals is anyone's guess.

As for those few pages that Pflock was allowed to see – and to transcribe word for word – they tell a tale of undeniable weirdness. By his own admittance, and a couple of years after the Aztec story surfaced in Frank Scully's book, Newton was clandestinely visited by two representatives of "a highly secret U.S. Government entity," as Pflock carefully and tactfully described it. Those same representatives of the government told Newton, in no uncertain terms, that they knew his Aztec story was a complete and bald-faced lie. Utter bullshit, in fact. Incredibly, though, they wanted Newton to *keep telling the tale* to just about anyone and everyone who would listen. This caused Pflock to ponder on an amazing possibility: "Did the U.S. Government or someone associated with it use Newton to discredit the idea of crashed flying saucers so a real captured saucer or saucers could be more easily kept under wraps?"

Far more intriguing, though, and highly relevant to the theme of this book, is the next question that Pflock posed: "Was this actually *nothing* to do with *real* saucers but instead *some sort of psychological warfare operation* [italics mine]?" With the Newton revelations in hand, Pflock, no later than 1999, came to believe that back in the early fifties someone in the government, the intelligence community, or the military of the United States – and maybe even a swirling combination of all three – wanted the Aztec story further circulated. The purpose: as a means to try and convince the Russians that the U.S. military had acquired, or captured, alien technology. When, in reality, it had no such thing in its possession at all.

For the record, in 2002, when Pflock and I were corresponding regularly on the matter of these particularly curious revelations, he told me that he had been able to confirm who the two men that approached Newton worked for and specifically when their meeting with Newton occurred.

The timeframe was late March 1950 and the pair of spooks came from a small group within the CIA. Slightly more than a year later, Pflock learned, that very same group was absorbed into the Psychological Strategy Board. Files on the PSB are held at the President Harry S. Truman Library & Museum. Its staff have prepared the following summary on the history and work of the PSB. It was established by Presidential Directive on April 4,

1951 "to authorize and provide for the more effective planning, coordination, and conduct within the framework of approved national policies, of psychological operations." An abbreviated version of the Presidential Directive was released to the public on June 20, 1951.

The PSB was composed of the Undersecretary of State, the Deputy Secretary of Defense and the Director of Central Intelligence, or their designated representatives. The founding Presidential Directive instructed the PSB to report to the National Security Council "on the Board's activities on the evaluation of the national psychological operations, including implementation of approved objectives, policies, and programs by the departments and agencies concerned."

The Psychological Strategy Board succeeded the State-War-Navy Coordinating Committee, which had been established during World War II to coordinate the Government's psychological warfare efforts. During the Truman Presidency, the PSB, in addition to its inherited coordination role, conducted planning for psychological operations undertaken by its constituent agencies. It did not conduct operations of its own. According to Edward P. Lilly, the PSB's historian, the Board's basic function was to prevent interagency rivalries from developing among the agencies involved in psychological operations. Seventeen meetings of the PSB's constituent agency representatives were held during the last year and a half of Truman's administration.

During the Eisenhower presidency, the PSB became purely a coordinating body; all planning was discontinued. The Board was terminated by Executive Order 10483 of

September 3, 1953, and its functions were transferred to
the Operations Coordinating Board.

Having digested the words above, it can be said with a high degree
of certainty that those predecessors to the PSB, which Newton
was confronted by, would have been the perfect people to have
enlisted Newton into their operation mind-fuck. Not only that,
in November 1998 Pflock secured from Bill Moore – co-author
with Charles Berlitz of the 1980 book, *The Roswell Incident* – a
copy of Newton's will. Having earlier seen Newton's "scrawling,
sprawling" writing up close at that Bernalillo restaurant, Pflock
said: "The will unquestionably is in Newton's hand, and while I'm
certainly not a handwriting expert, the comparison left no doubt
in my mind that he wrote the journal, too."

I know just how fascinated Pflock was when it came to the
Aztec crash and the claims of Newton and that "highly secret
U.S. Government entity." Pflock and I had been corresponding as
far back as the late 1990s, but, I didn't meet him in person until
2003 – at a UFO gig in the city of Aztec itself. For a number of
years, the conference was an annual event. But no more. Eclipsed
by Roswell? Probably. When Pflock and I finally met, he near-im-
mediately suggested that we should write an Aztec-themed book.
Pflock's reasoning was that he knew the story very well, and, via
the provisions of the Freedom of Information Act, I had uncovered hundreds upon hundreds of pages of material – chiefly from
the FBI – on the Aztec controversy and the players within it. He
thought that we would make a good team. Particularly so now
that I lived in the U.S. – and specifically in Dallas, Texas, which
(in terms of the road-trips that I regularly undertake) is not at all
far from New Mexico, where Pflock resided and where the 1948
crash supposedly happened.

As I listened, Pflock told me that his idea was, essentially, to make the book a biography on Newton, but with the Aztec affair being the main thrust of it all. I thought it was a very good idea. Pflock suggested that he prepare a synopsis for his literary agent, Cherry Weiner (this was around a year before I first met my longstanding agent, Lisa Hagan), which is exactly what he did. The book was going to be called *Silas the Magnificent: A True Tale of Greed, Credulity, and (Maybe) Government Chicanery and Cover-up in 1950s America.* Sadly, the idea collapsed when Pflock fell seriously ill with Amyotrophic Lateral Sclerosis, or Lou Gehrig's disease. He unfortunately died from the effects of ALS on June 5, 2006, at the age of just sixty-three. Pflock is gone, but the synopsis still exists, as do several chapters, including one on the matter of the Psychological Strategy Board aspect of all this. It would have made a good book. And, very possibly, it just might have revealed more of the fabricated story of how – and with the help of Silas Newton - American intelligence led the Russians on a wild goose chase and had them believing that U.S. scientists were secretly studying a recovered UFO and its advanced technologies and weapons-systems. If such a plot successfully terrified Soviet intelligence, for the U.S. government it was a job well done.

There's one more thing that needs to be highlighted on this controversy-saturated saga of a crashed UFO and Silas Newton. On June 24, 1964, Frank Scully, whose 1950 book, *Behind the Flying Saucers*, placed the alleged incident firmly under the spotlight, passed away. As the *New York Times* noted in its obituary on Scully, one day later: "Mr. Scully was labeled a Communist by Congressman Martin Dies, head of the House Un-American Activities Committee. After a stormy two-hour session with the Committee, Mr. Scully was cleared of the charge."

Yes, Scully was exonerated. It is a fact, though, that sometimes – to use a U.K. term – "mud sticks." For some, including those in the intelligence community, Scully was still seen as a closet communist, regardless of the fact that he had been completely absolved of any kind of guilt. Maybe, those spooks and spies who paid Silas Newton a visit in 1950 were concerned by the possibility that Scully was in cahoots with the Russians. This is, admittedly, speculation and nothing more. But, yet again, we see flying saucer enthusiasts, communism, and secret government activity rolled into one.

Nineteen-forty-eight was not just notable, in UFO terms, for the twisted tale of the supposed Aztec UFO crash. It was also the year in which a very intriguing novel was published. Its title was *The Flying Saucer* and its author was Bernard Newman. In some respects, the story that Newman weaved in 1948 closely mirrored the claims of Alfred O'Donnell in 2011, as they related to the Roswell controversy of July 1947. In the 250-pages of *The Flying Saucer*, we are treated to a tale of cover-ups, conspiracies, and fabricated tales of Martians and UFOs. The story revolves around a group of scientists who decide that the people of Earth need to be united under one banner. A one-world society. But how could such a thing be achieved? By creating a faked alien threat, that's how. (See what I mean about the O'Donnell parallels and his claims of a bogus UFO threat that led to the incident at Roswell, New Mexico just one year before Newman's novel was published?)

In *The Flying Saucer*, those aforementioned scientists decide to fake a trio of UFO crashes, as a means to convince the world that aliens have reached the Earth, and that those same scientists have the priceless evidence in their hands. One of those three incidents occurs in the heart of New Mexico, no less. Another UFO crashes in the Soviet Union, and a third slams into the ground in the U.K. Of course, the crashes are actually nothing of the sort. Rather, they are ingeniously staged events designed to make the world believe that the Martians are among us. Scientists create the futuristic aircraft, making them appear to have unearthly origins. The team even stages a bogus alien autopsy, as a means to even further convince people that we are not alone in the universe. The plan is to unite the human race under one friendly benevolent government. I'll let you learn for yourselves how the story develops and reaches its climax. It's not just the story that is intriguing – given that we now know such machinations were already afoot in the real world – but the author, Bernard Newman, himself, too.

Philip Taylor, a researcher who has dug deeply into the life and career of Bernard Newman, says: "In his unrevealing auto-biography *Speaking From Memory* [Newman] describes how from 1919 onwards he was apparently employed in an undemanding Civil Service job in the Ministry of Works. Somehow he seemed able to take extremely long and, for those days, exceedingly adventurous holidays, including lengthy stays in Eastern Europe and Russia. His destinations invariably seemed to include areas of particular political interest: for example several extended holidays to Germany in the 1930's."

Taylor also reveals that in 1938 Newman put together a paper for British Intelligence on the then-current state of German rock-etry at the Peenemünde Army Research Center. It was overseen by the German Army Weapons Office. It so happens that none other than the Horten Brothers - who, as we have seen, played a huge role in Alfred O'Donnel's claims concerning Roswell – witnessed a number of test-flights of the Messerschmitt ME 163 *Komet* aircraft at the Peenemünde Army Research Center. Yet another curious thread, then, is weaved into the story. But, things don't end there.

In 1945 the *New York Times* ran an article on Newman who, by that time, was a well-respected, prestigious author on matters relative to the world of espionage. Indeed, his books that were published before the *New York Times* article appeared included *The Secrets of German Espionage; Ride to Russia; Woman Spy;* and *Spy Catchers*. As for that same article, it addresses, in part, claims that Newman worked as a "double-agent" during the First World War, infiltrating the German military and securing some of the Germans' most prized secrets. This is not impossible, since Newman was fluent in German. He was, however, only eighteen at the time, which admittedly stretches credulity to a degree. On this matter, in February 1968, when Newman died, the U.K.'s *Times* newspaper suggested that this part of Newman's life should be relegated to "the realm of fiction."

We may never know for sure all that Bernard Newman learned during his life as a prestigious writer on the world of spying, espionage and counterintelligence. But, we do know that in 1948, only one year after the events outside of Roswell, New Mexico occurred, Newman wrote a novel - *The Flying Saucer* – which contained just about all of the key ingredients that comprise the primary themes of the book you are now reading: faked UFO crashes, a bogus alien invasion, and the manipulation of the mindset of the populace. One has to wonder if Newman - who cultivated numerous colleagues and friends in the intelligence community - heard and learned something akin to Alfred O'Donnell's claims and decided to turn startling fact into captivating fiction.

Now, let's jump four years forward.

For decades, tales have circulated suggesting that in 1952 a flying saucer crashed on the island of Spitsbergen, Norway. And, that under circumstances not dissimilar to those that supposedly occurred at Aztec, New Mexico, in 1948, the unearthly craft was supposedly recovered, along with its deceased alien crew. It transpires that a reference to this case can be found in a UFO-themed document that has surfaced under the terms of the U.S. Freedom of Information Act from the National Security Agency. It's a reference that adds yet further weight to the idea that government operatives have carefully and clandestinely used the UFO subject for manipulative, mind-warping purposes.

The NSA's copy of this previously-classified document is very slightly different to copies of the same document that have been declassified by the U.S. Air Force, the Department of State, and the U.S. Army. Someone in the NSA – unfortunately, we don't know who – identified the Spitsbergen story in the document as being a "plant." As for who secretly seeded the story, and why, well, that's another matter entirely. Maybe, U.S. intelligent agents planted the story to try and further have the Russians believe that the U.S. government was back-engineering extraterrestrial space-craft when it really wasn't. On the other hand, the "planters" may have been the Soviets themselves, trying to achieve something almost identical, but aimed squarely at the heart of the White House and the Pentagon.

Jack Brewer, who runs *The UFO Trail* blog, says of all this amazing chicanery concerning the Spitsbergen saucer saga of 1952: "It should be a forgone conclusion at this point that the UFO topic was exploited by the global intelligence community for a variety of purposes from one operation and era to the next. The consequences might indeed be significant and far-reaching."

From 1947 to the early years of the 1950s, we have seen prime evidence of how the East and the West used the UFO phenomenon – the "mythos" might be a more appropriate word to use – as a means to put the wind up the opposition. As will become clear in the following chapter, not only did these programs continue; they also resulted in the creation of some seriously weird, and highly influential, belief-systems concerning extraterrestrials. In some quarters, they still continue to be championed to this very day.

5.

"THE EXPLOITATION OF SUPERSTITIONS"

Briefly moving matters away from UFOs – but still in connection to issues of both a supernatural and a paranormal type – there is another example of how both the Russians and the United States, in the early 1950s, came to realize how the world of the unknown could be used for military gain and psychological manipulation. The story is found in the pages of a fascinating document written on April 14, 1950. The author was Jean M. Hungerford, of the RAND Corporation. Her report was prepared for the U.S. Air Force. For those not acquainted with the work of RAND, there is the following from the corporation itself:

"In May 14, 1948, Project RAND—an organization formed immediately after World War II to connect military planning with research and development decisions— separated from the Douglas Aircraft Company of Santa Monica, California, and became an independent, nonprofit organization. Adopting its name from a contraction of the term *research and development*, the newly formed entity was dedicated to furthering and promoting scientific, educational, and charitable purposes for the public welfare and security of the United States.

"Almost at once, RAND developed a unique style. It blended scrupulous nonpartisanship with rigorous fact-based analysis to tackle society's most pressing problems. Over time, RAND assembled a unique corps of researchers, notable not only for their individual skills but also for their commitment to interdisciplinary cooperation. By the 1960s, RAND was bringing its trademark mode of empirical, nonpartisan, independent analysis to the study of many urgent domestic social and economic problems. In later years, RAND extended its focus beyond the United States with the goal of making individuals, communities, and nations safer and more secure, healthier and more prosperous."

The title of Jean M. Hungerford's 1950 document for RAND was: *The Exploitation of Superstitions for Purposes of Psychological Warfare.* Running to thirty-seven pages, Hungerford's paper reveals – in brilliant fashion – just how easy it really was to use paranormal phenomena to affect the enemy to an extraordinary degree. Hungerford wrote: "Recently a series of religious 'miracles' has been reported from Czechoslovakian villages. In one instance the cross on the altar of a parish church was reported to have bowed right and left and finally, symbolically, to the West; the 'miracle' so impressed the Czechs that pilgrims began to converge on the village from miles around until Communist officials closed the church and turned the pilgrims away from approaching roads."

As Hungerford also revealed, rumors were flying around those same areas that the Virgin Mary had been seen confronting an unknown communist - and, in the process, whacking him to the ground! From Western Bohemia, another story surfaced: that the Virgin Mary had been seen proudly flying the flag of the United States, while American soldiers and tanks dutifully followed her.

There's no doubt at all that this was a well-crafted piece of U.S.-created mind-manipulation, designed to try and convince those of a communist nature that the Virgin Mary was on the side of the Land of the Free. That was not the end of the matter, though.

Jean M. Hungerford added in her RAND document that U.S. intelligence took a very careful note of what the Russians' and the Czechs' responses were to these incredible claims. The American military quietly – and very carefully - listened in on radio-based broadcasts and quickly got all the data they needed to know. That the Russians and the Czechs were mightily angry with those claims of the Virgin Mary being pro-American. Hungerford added: "According to the Foreign Broadcast Information Services' daily reports of Soviet and Eastern European radio broadcasts, there were nine broadcasts concerning the 'miracles' between February 28 and March 19, seven from Czech transmitters and two from Moscow (including a review of a *New Times* article on the subject)."

The CIA, Hungerford revealed, translated a Prague-based on-air broadcast about the controversy-filled situation. Obviously, the CIA was as keen as the U.S. Air Force to see just how successfully the program was working. In part, the translation read as follows: "It is obvious at first sight that this apparition bears the mark made in the United States. These despicable machinations only help to unmask the high clergy as executors of the plans of the imperialist warmongers communicated to them by the Vatican through its agents."

In this case there was not a UFO in sight. What there was, however, was an impressively- created tale of a supernatural entity – the Virgin Mary – that was designed to disrupt the Russians. Which it did. To ever-growing degrees, agencies were coming to see just how far they could go when it came to blending intelligence operations, propaganda and espionage with the world of the paranormal. Now, let's take a look at another portion of

Hungerford's report which most assuredly *does* have a connection to UFOs – and also to how the phenomenon could be used for highly alternative reasons.

In one part of *The Exploitation of Superstitions for Purposes of Psychological Warfare*, Jean M. Hungerford discusses a book that was written in the previous year, 1949. The title of that book was *Magic: Top Secret*. Its author was a man, magician and military figure named Jasper Maskelyne. The *Magic Tricks* website says this of Maskelyne: "Jasper Maskelyne, grandson of John Nevil Maskelyne, was an invaluable resource to his native Britain during World War II. Maskelyne became an integral part of a special unit focused on the action along the Suez Canal. With his great knowledge of illusion, Maskelyne was able to devise ingenious- and very large scale- illusion systems that virtually made tanks invisible from the air, hid whole buildings full of ammunition and supplies, and even made an entire city vanish and reappear several miles away."

Hungerford, in her RAND paper for the U.S. Air Force, made an eye-catching quote from Maskelyne's book. That same quote reads as follows: "Our men…were able to use illusions of an amusing nature in the Italian mountains, especially when operating in small groups as advance patrols scouting out the way for our general moves forward. In one area, in particular, they used a device which was little more than a gigantic scarecrow, about twelve feet high, and able to stagger forward under its own power and emit frightful flashes and bangs. This thing scared several Italian Sicilian villages appearing in the dawn thumping its deafening way down their streets with great electric blue sparks jumping from it; and the inhabitants, who were mostly illiterate peasants, simply took to their heels for the next village, swearing that the Devil was marching ahead of the invading English.

"Like all tales spread among uneducated folk (and helped, no doubt, by our agents), this story assumed almost unimaginable proportions. Villages on the route of our advance began to refuse sullenly to help the retreating Germans, and to take sabotage against them; and then, instead of waiting for our troops to arrive with food and congratulations of their help, the poor people fled, thus congesting the roads along which German motorized transport was struggling to retire. The German tankmen sometimes cut through the refugees and this inflamed feeling still more, and what began almost as a joke was soon a sharp weapon in our hands which punished the Germans severely, if indirectly, for several critical weeks."

It's important to note that the description of Jasper Maskelyne's giant, sparking scarecrow sounds astonishingly like a famous alien monster that surfaced in the woods of West Virginia on the night of September 12, 1952. The glowing-eyed thing has become known in Ufology as the "Flatwoods Monster," after the small town where the creature was briefly seen by a terrified band of locals. Both Maskelyne's contraption and the creature of Flatwoods were around twelve-feet in height. Frank Feschino is the acknowledged expert on the Flatwoods Monster. The cover-art on his 2004 book – *The Braxton County Monster: The Cover-Up of the Flatwoods Monster Revealed* – shows a huge robot-like thing looming over a terrified group in a menacing fashion. Beams of light shoot out of its eyes. Maskelyne's machine was said to have emitted "frightful flashes and bangs" and had "great electric blue sparks jumping from it." Both "creatures" were seen in the vicinities of small towns, which would have made it easy for the military – in Italy during the Second World War and at Flatwoods in 1952 - to keep a stealthy watch on the situations and judge just how successfully, or not, the deceptive operations were working. The parallels between both accounts are as clear as they are blatantly obvious.

Could the U.S. Air Force have constructed its very own equivalent of Jasper Maskelyne's clunking device that struck terror into the hearts of Italian village folk during the Second World War? Possibly. The story was revealed in Maskelyne's book in 1949 and was shared with the Air Force one year later, thanks to Jean M. Hungerford. The Flatwoods Monster appeared – seemingly out of nowhere – in 1952, two years later. That would have been ample time for the Air Force to have created its own version of Maskelyne's monster. And to unleash it too, and have the people of Flatwoods believe it was an extraterrestrial creature.

And, finally, we should not overlook the major significance of the title of Jean M. Hungerford's paper: *The Exploitation of Superstitions for Purposes of Psychological Warfare*. The fact is that psychological warfare is at the heart of practically all of the cases under the microscope in this book. With that all said, it's now time to meet a man who claimed to have met aliens and who the FBI kept a close watch on. The motivation for the surveillance? That man's apparent love of Russia and communism. His name was George Adamski.

6.

"POWERFUL IMAGES BECOME PERMANENT FAST-BREEDERS"

Born in Poland in 1891, George Adamski – of *Flying Saucers Have Landed* notoriety - was the ultimate "contactee," regardless of what you may or may not think of him and his tales. He defined what it meant in the 1950s to have interactions with beings from other worlds; creatures very much like us and who wished us nothing but goodwill. Adamski's primary visitor from the great beyond was Orthon. Adamski's forays into the world of the supernatural, however, did not begin when the flying saucer phenomenon was at its height. Adamski had been involved in matters of a metaphysical type for *years*. For example, in April 1934, the *Los Angeles Times* ran a feature on the man himself with a headline that succinctly read as follows: "Shamanistic Order to be Established Here." In part, it states:

> "The 10-foot trumpets of faraway Lhasa, perched among perpetual snows in the Himalayan Mountains in Tibet, will shortly have their echo on the sedate hills of Southern California's Laguna Beach. Already the Royal Order of Tibet has acquired acreage on the placid hills that bathe their Sunkist feet in the purling Pacific and before long, the walls, temples, turrets and dungeons of a Lama monastery will serrate the skyline. It will be the first Tibetan

monastery in America and in course of time, the trained disciples of the cult will filter through its glittering gates to spread 'the ancient truths' among all who care to listen. The central figure in the new movement is Prof. George Adamski."

It's important to note that Adamski was *never* a professor. Of *anything*. But, he most certainly didn't mind the suggestion that he *was* a professor. He told the *Los Angeles Times*, in what was an undeniably pompous fashion: "I learned great truths up there on the roof of the world, or rather the trick of applying age-old knowledge to daily life, to cure the body and the mind, and to win mastery over self and soul. I do not bring to Laguna the weird rites and bestial superstition in which the old Lamaism is steeped, but the scientific portions of the religion."

Adam Gorightly and Greg Bishop say in their *"A" is for Adamski* book that: "During Prohibition, The Royal Order of Tibet secured a special license to produce wine, which some suggest was Adamski's main motivation for starting his mystical order to begin with." Old George was definitely well-known for his particular fondness for the grape. Now, it's time to head to 1952, when Adamski's involvement in Ufology really took off. Maybe literally. At least, for those who bought, and still buy, into his stories.

It was early on the morning of November 20, 1952. Adamski and his faithful secretary Lucy McGinnis drove to Blythe, California. This was not your average road-trip, however. Adamski, when telling the story to whoever would listen, claimed that the reason for hitting the road to Blythe had an astonishing purpose behind it: aliens dearly wanted to meet with the professor-who-wasn't. The pair soon met up with other characters in 1950s-era Ufology.

They included UFO enthusiasts Al and Betty Bailey, and George Hunt Williamson. The latter was a controversial contactee who crossed paths with the FBI on several occasions, most seriously in 1962. That was when Williamson was suspected by the Bureau of smuggling priceless Mexican artifacts of an historic and archaeological significance into the United States.

After refueling their vehicles and their stomachs, the gang then headed out to Parker, Arizona – where, Adamski said, he was absolutely sure that aliens were soon to put in an appearance. So the tale goes, that's exactly what happened. A huge, "cigar"-shaped UFO loomed into view, high in the skies above Parker. The amazed crew hit a dirt-road in hot pursuit of the mighty craft. Adamski and company were not the only ones who were looking for a close encounter. Adamski claimed that a squadron of U.S. Air Force planes was also after the aliens. The people from the stars almost effortlessly made a quick escape from the pursuing pilots.

It wasn't long before a much smaller flying saucer made its appearance before the astonished group. In an almost Old Testament-style fashion, the gleaming craft landed on a nearby mountain, awaiting the disciple-like Adamski to come forward and meet his superior. He somehow knew that the aliens had come for him. Adamski approached the craft, while the rest – their mouths no doubt agape – looked on. An extremely-human-looking extraterrestrial exited the futuristic craft, just as Michael Rennie's character of Klaatu did in the classic 1951 movie, *The Day the Earth Stood Still*. Unlike Klaatu, though, Adamski's alien – who announced himself as Orthon – had long hair of the kind that just about any and every 1980s-era "hair-metal" rock band would have been proud to sport.

Orthon announced to Adamski that he came from Venus - and that he came in peace, too. In no time at all, Orthon began lecturing Adamski on why we, the human race, needed to ditch our atomic weapons. If we didn't, the only outcome would be overwhelming, worldwide destruction. Not only that, Orthon wanted Adamski to be one of the key figures in the plan to save the Earth and its people. In an instant, Adamski was up for the challenge. Orthon, seemingly happy with the outcome, returned to his flying saucer and shot off into the skies. An alien had come and gone, and for Adamski a new life had just begun. It was a life that both Russia and communism played a significant role in, which we will get to in the next chapter. But before we do so, let's take a closer look at Adamski, the man and the contactee combined.

There's no doubt that George Adamski was at the height of his fame from the early-to-mid 1950s, with the absolute peak year being 1953. That was when his book, *Flying Saucers Have Landed*, was published. It sold more than 100,000 copies in the process. The book was curious not just because of its content – controversial encounters with human-like aliens – but also because of how it was written. And by whom. It was credited to Adamski and an Irish writer named Desmond Leslie. That's not entirely wrong; but it's important to note that it's not precisely correct, either. It so happens that in the same time-fame that Adamski was toiling on his book, Leslie was working on a publication on strange phenomena in the skies: UFOs. Leslie got his hands on sixty pages of a manuscript on Adamski's claimed encounters that he, Adamski, had cobbled together in somewhat chaotic fashion. An agreement was made to combine the two works-in-progress and fuse them into one, which is exactly what happened. The reality, though, is that those sixty pages were not written by Adamski at all. They were actually *ghost*-written by Adamski's secretary, Lucy McGinnis. Adamski dictated the story to McGinnis, who made the whole thing readable, if not particularly believable.

On this issue of believability, or of a significant lack of it, we need to return to the words of the Gorightly-Bishop team: "*Flying Saucers Have Landed* wasn't Adamski's first stab at literary immortality. In the 1940s, he submitted a science-fiction yarn called 'Pioneers of Space' to *Amazing Stories* that featured an extraterrestrial messianic figure who comes to Earth bearing a message of peace and love. Adamski later self-published a book version of *Pioneers of Space* that fell by the wayside until debunkers rediscovered the work and pointed to it as an early fictional account of his Orthon encounter."

To fully understand the mindset of George Adamski, his motivations, and how he ultimately became a figure of concern and controversy to the FBI, we have to turn our attentions to Colin Bennett. He was the author of an excellent, illuminating biography on Adamski, *Looking for Orthon.* I also interviewed him on Adamski, his motivations, and his claims of alien encounters. Bennett shared the following thoughts and observations with me. They collectively suggest Adamski may actually have had some genuine alien encounters, but chose to combine the nature of those encounters with his personal admiration for communism and the Russians. Not a good idea.

Bennett said: "Many Orthons have appeared throughout history. The equivalents to Adamski's Venusian 'space brother' have appeared on mountain tops, in deserts, and have appeared to walk on water, or fly in the sky. Their sole function is to sow seeds in the head; just as a farmer grows a particular crop. These seeds act on the imagination, which replicates and amplifies whatever story-technology is around at the time. People such as Adamski and the rest of the contactees were, and still are, like psychic lightning-rods for certain brands of information. Undoubtedly, rich or poor, clever or dumb, they are possessed by a kind of higher cerebral disturbance, and, like Moses, they are as prepared for the 'visitation' as they anxiously await for a new product brand.

"Contactees are host-nutrients for whatever cultural sales lines are on offer from visions conjured up by clouds, sea or sand. The message is 'consumed' and thoroughly processed exactly as a viral product is absorbed. The incomprehensibility of the received stories is irrelevant. They represent a heavily codified branch of postmodern intellectual consumerism. In receiving 'messages' at all, Contactees are bar coded as it were, and elements of the induced story-technology are ready to crystallize out into that final alchemical stage called the mechanical real. But we must be careful here. As the alchemist said to his apprentice, 'The game may be rigged, but it's the only game in town.'

"Deception and all its ramifications is the key to this whole business. This does not burst the bubble of the mystery however, for manipulative levels of faction may well be our first clue as to how a possible alien mind might work. If the levels of deception of all kinds in human culture are anything to go by, the range of such within an alien culture must be both multiple and profound.

"The 'space-folk' are sculptured by wars between rival viral memes competing for prime-time belief. It may be that, as an independent form of non-organic life, memes as active viral information can display an Orthon entity at a drop of a hat. They come complete with sets of cultural agendas. After they have rung the doorbell as it were, and the goods are sold, these metaphysical salesmen disappear like the traditional Men in Black, no doubt traveling on to seed other dreams in other towns and other heads. The goods we have unwittingly bought are half-formed memories of having met someone from another world.

"Over a half-century later, we can no more erase the legendary Contactees from our heads than we can erase Elvis Presley or Marilyn Monroe. Once induced by mere transient suggestion, these powerful images become permanent fast-breeders, turning out scripts and performances in all our heads – for no one can escape – even as we sleep. It might come as a disappointment to extraterrestrial nut-and-bolters, but as [Jacques] Vallee says in *Passport to Magonia*, Orthon and his brood may be a form of 'alien' life that has been with us for a long time. Such ethereal beings are part of the structure of that much-despised and rather unfashionable idea described by the phrase mystical experience.

"A man says he has seen a fairy being. Another man says that is impossible, because fairy beings do not exist. When we subtract the two beliefs we do not get zero as an answer. We have the thinnest of belief-tissue remaining, but perhaps mechanical quantity is irrelevant. The smallest part of an HTML address contains the whole address, rather like a fractal. These creatures, though seen and photographed, leave no trace of fights, no food swath, no blood, no sweat. They appear as partially formed displays rather than flesh and blood as we know it. As soon as we are into display we are into Media. It is somewhat chilling to think that if an Orthon or even perhaps a Jesus can appear in this manner, then so can many things else, including objects and even situations. In this it is possible that we are host-receptors of skunk-smoke from life forms not yet known to us.

"There is no doubt that Contactee claims allow access to a refreshing world which includes humor, and inspired absurdity. They allow humanity to breathe and access a Matrix world in which anything that can be imagined can happen. It might be denied by social-scientific left, but the truth is that dreams, fantasies, and mystical experiences of all kinds play an absolutely essential part in all human mental operations.

"George Adamski played a significant part in establishing New Age thinking. It might be well to remember that the entire body of our moral philosophy and spiritual life is formed by visions and inspirations. It does not come from science or technology. Those who thoughtlessly dismiss mystical experience cut themselves off from all art, literature, and no small part of all thought and philosophy. As mystics and prophets know, when desert light strikes the retina, anything that can be imagined can happen. The greatest tribute that can be paid to Adamski is that through both foul means and fair, he helped to create one of the very few routes to the unconscious that we have."

Now, we have the words of the late Jim Moseley, who was a long-time observer of the UFO phenomenon. He was also someone who had the opportunity to chat, in person, with Adamski in 1953 about his claimed encounters: "When I met him," Moseley told me, "Adamski was in his guru mode. You could go to him at Palomar without an appointment and he would be sitting there, holding court, and talking to all the people that came in. He seemed like a pleasant sort. He couldn't prove anything; you had the choice of believing him or not. Now, whether he was genuine or not, he did have a background with the Royal Order of Tibet. Then, he wrote his science-fiction story, *Pioneers from*

Space, which turned out to be very similar to his later UFO book. I don't think he literally believed everything he said. *But, I think what he said was in-line with a personal philosophy that he may very well have taken seriously* [italics mine]. I think with Adamski it was like this: if I say 'I'm Jim Moseley, and I believe in world peace, love, and saving the environment,' people won't care. But, if I say that a spaceman called Orthon told me that we should love each other, well, that certainly gives it more meaning.

> "I think this is one of the big things behind the Contactee movement: they believed in what they were saying, but they needed a higher authority to get it across. Like in religion, you need God. Adamski needed Orthon. Adamski and the Contactees represented an early hippie philosophy of the time – a 1950s version of what came later in the Sixties with flower-power protests. A lot of what they were saying merged into the mainstream of liberal thinking at that time. So, in that way, it was a very significant movement."

7.

"RUSSIA WILL DOMINATE THE WORLD"

Having studied how George Adamski was elevated to astonishing levels of fame, infamy and notoriety, it's now time to address the matter of why, exactly, the FBI came to suspect that Adamski was not only a closet communist, but possibly even someone who was being used by the Russians in a strange psychological warfare-based operation. Just maybe, Adamski was an unwitting player in this strange and sinister game. In a worst-case scenario, though, Adamski was a knowing and entirely complicit figure. Certainly, the FBI wanted answers and, as a result, they dug very deeply into the man's life. As evidence of this, close to 400-pages of FBI documentation on Adamski have now been declassified. An FBI document of May 28, 1952 reveals that Bureau agents had a credible source who, back in 1950 – no less than three years before *Flying Saucers Have Landed* was published - had shared with them certain disturbing data on Adamski. The FBI took – and to this day continues to take – careful steps to ensure that its source's name would not be compromised.

What we *do* know is that the FBI's informant claimed to have seen Adamski in the presence of a group of Russians in downtown Los Angeles, California, on several occasions in 1950. Discussing politics, no less. Unfortunately, the available censored papers don't specify where exactly in L.A. the meetings occurred, or under what particular circumstances. Nor do we know who was responsible for the source of the story. Also, we have to wonder how the source was so absolutely certain that the group were Russians. Was he or she conversant in Russian? Did the source recognize the accent? Were they themselves Russian, too? If so, what were *they* doing in Los Angeles? On this specific part of the story, a lot of questions remain frustratingly and tantalizingly unanswered. I have to wonder if the Bureau's source may have slightly embellished this part of the story, as a means to try and justify further, deeper surveillance of Adamski. I should stress, though, that there is not a shred of evidence to suggest that the source exaggerated the story in the slightest; it's just a theory on my part. Also, lying to the FBI would have been a very stupid and reckless thing to do. We only have to take a look at certain events surrounding the undeniable Russian meddling of the past few years to see how lying to the Feds will get a person into deep, deep trouble. And even a significant number of years in the slammer. Minus your hair-dye, as per Paul Manafort.

With that said, let's now take a careful look at the contents of the most important portion of that inflammatory document, which makes it *very* clear that Adamski and communism went together, hand-in-glove.

> On September 5, 1950, [source] advised the San Diego Office that he first met Adamski about three months ago at the café which is named the Palomar Gardens Café, owned and operated by Adamski, at the road junction, five miles East of Rincon, California, at a point where the highway branches off leading to Mount Palomar Observatory. [Source] advised that Adamski has four or five women working in the café and according to [source] business does not warrant the employment of four or

five persons. [Source] stated that on August 20, 1950, the occasion of his last visit to Adamski's café, he [source] and a [deleted] of San Diego, became involved in a lengthy conversation with Adamski during which Adamski told them at great length of his findings of flying saucers and so forth. He told them of a space ship which he said he saw between the earth and the moon, which he estimated to be approximately three miles in length, which was flying so fast that he had to take about eighty photographs before he could get three of them to turn out.

At this time, Adamski showed [source] and [deleted] a number of photographs which he has taken of what he purports to be flying saucers. [Source] commented that one of these photographs was published in the "San Diego Union" under the caption of "What is it?" Adamski stated he had first submitted this particular photograph to the Navy but when it appeared they were not interested, he, Adamski, released it for publication in the 'San Diego Union.'

According to [source] Adamski stated that the Federal Communications Commission, under the direction of the "Military Government" of the United States, has established communication with the people from other worlds, and has learned that they are so much more advanced than the inhabitants of this earth that they have deciphered the languages used here. Adamski stated that in this interplanetary communication, the Federal Communications Commission asked the inhabitants of the other planet concerning the type of government they had there and the reply indicated that it was very different from the democracy of the United States. Adamski stated that his answer was kept secret by the United States Government, but he added, *'If you ask me they probably have a Communist form of government and our American government wouldn't release that kind of thing, naturally. That is a thing of the future – more advanced* [Authors note: Italics mine].

This, of course, was all highly controversial for the FBI of the early 1950s; highly worrying too. It's very easy to understand why the FBI would have taken such a deep interest in Adamski's opinions on extraterrestrials and communism. Of greater concern, however, was the fact that Adamski's followers - which reached six figures in number after his 1953 book, *Flying Saucers Have Landed* was published - were hanging on his every word. That included those words that were relative to the way of the life of the Russians. The FBI file continues:

Adamski, during this conversation, made the prediction that Russia will dominate the world and we will then have an era of peace for 1,000 years [italics mine]. He stated that Russia already has the atom bomb and the hydrogen bomb and that the great earthquake, which was reported behind the Iron Curtain recently, was actually a hydrogen bomb explosion being tried out by the Russians. Adamski states this "earthquake" broke seismograph machines and he added that no normal earthquake can do that.

Adamski stated that within the next twelve months, San Diego will be bombed. Adamski stated that it does not make any difference if the United States has more atom bombs than Russia inasmuch as Russia needs only ten atom bombs to cripple the United States by placing these simultaneously on such spots as Chicago and other vital centers of this country [italics mine]. Adamski further stated the United States today is in the same state of deterioration as was the Roman Empire prior to its collapse and it will fall just as the Roman Empire did. He stated the Government in this country is a corrupt form of government and capitalists are enslaving the labor.

[Source] advised that when Adamski left the group for a brief period, one of the women working in the café came over and entered into the conversation. She stated that some of our servicemen who stopped there to have drinks during World War II and subsequent thereto, told "Professor" Adamski of the atrocities which they were forced to commit, murdering women and children on orders of their superior officers. [Deleted] exhibited a great deal of animosity against the United States, stating the United States committed more atrocities during World War II than did the Japanese but since the Japanese were the ones who lost the war, they were the ones who were tried as war criminals.

This woman added that a friend of hers who recently returned from Russia stated he was very pleased with everything he found there. He stated to her that the people in Russia received seven tickets per month for the opera and cinema. These tickets are free, being issued by the government. The woman added *"The people there (in Russia) don't have to be worrying about where their next meal is coming from. Everything is fine in Russia and in the United States we have to fight for everything we get* [italics mine]. *"*

And if that was not enough, there's this:

[Source] advised that Adamski returned to continue his conversation stating that the United States will soon be in the same condition that Europe was in during the last war. He added that, "It is a good idea to be quiet now. Right now if you talk in favor of Communism you will be spotted as a Communist and if you talk against Communism you will be spotted by the Communist, so it's best to just shut up." Adamski stated to [source] that, *"The United States hasn't a chance to win the war. Russia will take over the United States* [italics mine]."

This was all deeply vexing to the FBI, to the extent that Adamski was from thereon closely, and secretly, watched for the best part of a decade. And, it was very much a learning process for the FBI, who discovered that communism and the Contactee issue were not limited to just Adamski. To the consternation of the FBI, they quickly discovered that numerous other Contactees were rumored to have had Red leanings, and/or connections, as will soon become apparent. I asked Colin Bennett for his thoughts on the matter of Adamski, the FBI, and the Russian/communist issue. He said:

"The FBI regarded Adamski as little more than a pop-eyed hippy nutcase – *at first*. He was, however, beginning to get a certain following, and he was watched as -- much later -- John Lennon, Timothy Leary, Andrija Puharich, and Wilhelm Reich were watched. We can assume all possible cult followers, right up to the present day are taken note of in a similar manner. To begin with, the flying saucer bit probably did not interest the FBI at all, even if they knew, cared, or understood anything about such things. Until, now we know, his book-sales skyrocketed and then someone in the FBI went back to the 1950 files on him and saw how he mixed saucers, Nazism and communism. Then, they *did* take notice. He did not make a big thing of such opinions, publicly, during the [Second World] War, but he certainly voiced them after the War, at a time when hundreds of thousands of American dead were fresh in the memory, and that could not have gone down well. He was ripe for investigation.

"Another level of Intelligence interest," opined Bennett, "might have been aroused concerning possible observation of unusual airborne devices which might well have been advanced secret surveillance craft of some kind, possibly launched from Russian submarines off the West Coast. There was also another good reason for suspicion. In the 1950s, myriad tests were being carried out on jets, rockets and missiles in the Mojave Desert where Orthon appeared originally. Many of these tests were carried out by imported Nazis rocket-scientists and technological experts, secretly smuggled into the U.S. by means of Operation Paperclip. Intelligence surveillance in this area was therefore high, for by 1953, the race for the moon had just commenced. Reports of exotic airborne vehicles may well have leaked from the Mojave area and created all kinds of 'alien craft' rumors."

Bennett continued with the following:

"Yet another reason for surveillance of Adamski was that security agencies of any and every kind operate on the principle that cults can turn political very quickly, and often in a very nasty way. As we know, countless assassins and terrorists arise from cults of many kinds. Official interest, to my mind, was therefore a passing criminal interest, not an esoteric one; although Adamski in his semi-paranoid act as a rather comical anarchist tried to make it so, implying all kinds of motivations to even minimal gumshoe levels of official inquiry. It must be remembered that before he became a famous author with a best-selling book, he was the kind of guy who sounded off about anything and everything. His murky 'occult' involvements with the esoteric underground on the wild West Coast between the time of his youth in World War One and the 1950s marked him out as a very odd character indeed.

"I asked myself: why should we – and the FBI - be so alarmed by a man who says he met a supposed extra-terrestrial being who stepped out of a so-called flying saucer? Why should such a man be regarded as a threat and be ridiculed for his trouble?"

Bennett answered his own questions:

"It appears that certain kinds of fantastic claims, no matter how apparently ridiculous and plain stupid, somehow get to the core of our belief system – and they can change conventional belief-systems, which the FBI knew and feared most of all. Claims push aside momentarily all plain practical rationalizations and thoroughly disturb our iron-bound consciousness. Most structured, factual arguments just do not have this kind of power."

Bennett signed off with these words:

"Adamski, whether he really realized it or not, had immense power. Potentially. The FBI, while not believing his tales and adventures of Orthon, recognized that potential power; *a power to manipulate the masses in a way that suggested*

Communism was not a thing to fear [italics mine]. It appears that all things out of the ordinary are potential mental dynamite – and, for [J. Edgar] Hoover, that included Adamski's claims of Red spacemen dabbling in our affairs, and Russian superiority."

8.

"MAJJ HYJTERIA AND GREATER VULNERABILITY"

Moving on from matters relative to George Adamski, aliens and communism, it's now time to take a look at the strange saga of flying saucers, the CIA, the Soviets, and the Walt Disney Corporation. Yes, you *did* read the correct. And, no, it's *not* April Fools' Day. Ward Kimball was a significant figure in the Walt Disney Corporation. His biggest claim to fame? Kimball created none other than Mickey Mouse, in the form he appears today. Kimball came on-board with Disney in the mid-1930s and worked on a number of timeless, acclaimed movies, including *Peter Pan*, *Pinocchio*, and *Snow White*, to list just a few. That's not all: for a while Kimball had a secret life; it was one of almost cloak-and-dagger proportions. Back in the 1950s, he and a number of his colleagues at Disney worked on a CIA-driven operation, the goal of which was to try and diffuse the Russians' attempts to use the UFO phenomenon to create mayhem in the United States. To understand how and why this very weird affair came to fruition we have to go back to the summer of 1952.

On the weekend of July 19-20, 1952, Washington, D.C. was swamped with squadrons of what can only be termed as UFOs: they were seen by both military and civilian pilots, reported by police officers, and tracked by astounded radar operatives at several airports in the D.C. area. Strange and fast moving lights dominated the airspace of the U.S. capital. Mystifying aerial acrobatics filled the night sky. It wasn't exactly *The Day the Earth Stood Still* come to reality, but it was pretty damn close all the same. Such was the sheer scale of the "invasion," the U.S. Air Force took swift and decisive action to try and resolve the matter. They had barely begun to try and figure out what had happened – and who or what had intruded on that dark night – when the UFOs were back, exactly a week later. The USAF's Major General John A. Samford wrote in a classified document the following: "We are interested in these reports in that we must always be on the alert for any threat or indication of a threat to the United States. *We cannot ignore these reports but the mild hysteria subsequent to publicity given this subject caused an influx of reports which since the 19th of July has almost saturated our 'Emergency' procedures* [italics mine]." Yet again, we see concerns regarding "hysteria" when it comes to UFOs in the early years of the Cold War. And also worries about endless UFO reports swamping emergency communications.

A two-page Air Force summary of what had gone down on the second weekend provides significant insight into the disturbing intrusion:

> This incident involved unidentified targets observed on the radar-scopes at the Air Route Traffic Control Center and the tower, both at Washington National Airport, and the Approach Control Radar at Andrews Air Force Base. Mr. Bill Schreve, flying a/c NC-12 reported at 22:46 EDT that he had visually spotted 5 objects giving off a light glow ranging from orange to white; his altitude at time was 2,200'. Some commercial pilots reported visuals ranging from 'cigarette glow' to a "light."
>
> ARTC crew commented that, as compared with returns picked up in early hours of 20 July 52, these

returns appeared to be more haphazard in their actions, i.e. they did not follow a/c around nor did they cross scope consistently on same general heading. Some commented that the returns appeared to be from objects "capable of dropping out of the pattern at will." Also that returns had "creeping appearance." One member of crew commented that one object to which F-94 was vectored just "disappeared from Scope" shortly after the F-94 started pursuing. All crew members emphatic that most returns have been picked up from time to time over the past few months but never before had they appeared in such quantities over such a prolonged period and with such definition as was experienced on the nights of 19/20 and 26/27 July 1952.

Further data concerning the invasions can be found in a recorded conversation of July 26, between staff at Washington National Airport and radar operators at Andrews Air Force Base, Maryland:

Washington: Andrews Tower, do you read? Did you have an airplane in sight west-northwest or east of your airport eastbound?

Andrews: No, but we just got a call from the Center. We're looking for it.

Washington: We've got a big target showing up on our scope. He's just coming in on the west edge of your airport – the northwest edge of it eastbound. He'll be passing right through the northern portion of your field on an east heading. He's about a quarter of a mile from the northwest runway – right over the edge of your runway now.

Andrews: This is Andrews. Our radar tracking says he's got a big fat target out here northwest of Andrews. He says he's got two more south of the field.

Washington: Yes, well the Center has about four or five around the Andrews Range Station. The Center is working a National Airlines – the Center is working him and vectoring him around his target. He went around Andrews. He saw one of them – looks like a meteor… went by him…or something. He said he's got one about three miles off his right wing right now. There are so many targets around here it is hard to tell as they are not moving very fast.

It wasn't just the Air Force who was getting antsy and worried by the invasions. The FBI was determined to get the facts, too. It was pretty much inevitable that word would trickle down to the office of J. Edgar Hoover. As we have seen, the FBI played a significant role in the flying saucer saga in 1947, and just a few years later with regard to George Adamski and his pro-Russia words. Hoover wasted no time in ordering the FBI's USAF liaison representative – N.W. Philcox – to secure all of the salient facts on the D.C. penetrations. On July 29, Philcox contacted the office of the Director of Air Intelligence - who at the time was Major General John A. Samford - to arrange a face-to-face discussion with Commander Randall Boyd, who was attached to the Current Intelligence Branch, Estimates Division, Air Intelligence, on the matter of "the present status of Air Intelligence research into the numerous reports regarding flying saucers and flying discs."

Given the fact that the media and the public quickly learned of the incredible scale of the two "weekend waves," the Air Force put out a statement to the effect that it was nothing to be concerned about. Of course, that was just a diversionary tactic on the part of the military; an attempt to avoid creating public concern on a large scale. Behind the scenes, however, the situation was very different. At the very same time that the press were being encouraged to move along and forget those strange, few nights of craziness, the Air Force was privately displaying a high degree of unease. In a classified meeting Philcox was told that, "at the present time the Air Force has failed to arrive at any satisfactory conclusion in its research regarding numerous reports of flying saucers and flying discs sighted throughout the United States." He was also advised that staff at Wright-Patterson Air Force Base, Dayton, Ohio were busy "coordinating, correlating and making research into all reports regarding flying saucers and flying discs."

It was also explained to Philcox that there were three definable categories of flying saucer reports. The first was that which revolved around encounters that "are reported by citizens who claim they have seen flying saucers from the ground. These sightings vary in description, color and speeds. Very little credence is given to these sightings inasmuch as in most instances they are believed to be imaginative or some explainable object which actually crossed through the sky."

As for category two, the following statement was made to Philcox: "Sightings reported by commercial or military pilots. These sightings are considered more credible by the Air Force inasmuch as commercial or military pilots are experienced in the air and are not expected to see objects which are entirely imaginative. In each of these instances, the individual who reports the sightings is thoroughly interviewed by a representative of Air Intelligence so that a complete description of the object can be obtained."

Then, there was the third group. Commander Boyd admitted to Philcox that the Air Force had highly credible reports on file; ones which involved sightings of UFOs that were seen by pilots and tracked by radar operators – and at the same time and in the same location. In his write-up to J. Edgar Hoover, Philcox wrote: "Commander Boyd advised that this latter classification constitutes two or three per cent of the total number of sightings, but that they are the most credible reports received and are difficult to explain. In these instances, there is no doubt that these individuals reporting the sightings actually did see something in the sky. Sightings have also recently been reported as far distant as Acapulco, Mexico, Korea and French Morocco…the sightings reported in the last classification have never been satisfactorily explained."

Incredibly, Philcox told his FBI boss that "[Boyd] advised that it is not entirely impossible that the objects may possibly be ships from another planet such as Mars."

The CIA – inevitably – also expressed a great deal of concern in relation to this particular issue. The agency had secretly monitored the UFO phenomenon since 1947, the year in which the flying saucer phenomenon began and the CIA was created. Like the Air Force, the CIA chose to do their utmost to play down the seriousness of the situation. But, it wasn't just UFO encounters that perturbed the agency. The CIA's finest were particularly troubled by the scenario of the Russians spreading bogus tales of invading aliens and plunging the American people into a state of nationwide terror. And, on top of that, of the Russians' actions leading to a potential jamming of U.S. emergency services – which could have been disastrous for the United States, had the Russians chose to launch a sneak attack. For months afterwards, the CIA debated on how best to try and prevent any such situation from occurring. It was on December 2, 1952 that the CIA's Assistant Director H. Marshall Chadwell stated the following to the agency's hierarchy: "Sightings of unexplained objects at great altitudes and traveling at high speeds in the vicinity of major U.S. defense installations are of such nature that they are not attributable to natural phenomena or known types of aerial vehicles."

Chadwell did more than that; he prepared the following for the National Security Council:

1. The Director of Central Intelligence shall formulate and carry out a program of intelligence and research activities as required to solve the problem of instant positive identification of unidentified flying objects.

2. Upon call of the Director of Central Intelligence, Government departments and agencies shall provide assistance in this program of intelligence and research to the extent of their capacity provided, however, that the DCI shall avoid duplication of activities presently directed toward the solution of this problem.

3. This effort shall be coordinated with the military services and the Research and Development Board of the Department of Defense, with the Psychological Board and other Governmental agencies as appropriate.

4. The Director of Central Intelligence shall disseminate information concerning the program of intelligence and research activities in this field to the various departments and agencies which have authorized interest therein.

Two days later, the Intelligence Advisory Committee agreed with Chadwell's plans and made a recommendation that "the services of selected scientists to review and appraise the available evidence in the light of pertinent scientific theories" should be employed.

It was as a direct outcome of this development that what became known as the Robertson Panel was created; a group headed by Howard Percy Robertson, who was a highly respected consultant to the Agency. He was also a noted physicist, and the director of the Defense Department Weapons Evaluation Group.

It was Chadwell's job to select a group of individuals who were deemed to be the right people to tackle the UFO problem – which included anxieties concerning Russian propaganda. The group included Luis Alvarez, physicist, radar expert (and later, a Nobel Prize recipient); Frederick C. Durant, CIA officer, secretary to the panel and missile expert; Samuel Abraham Goudsmit, Brookhaven National Laboratories nuclear physicist; and Thornton Page, astrophysicist, radar expert, and deputy director of Johns Hopkins Operations Research Office. In rapid time they plunged into the heart of the mystery.

There have been longstanding rumors in the field of Ufology that the CIA knows all about the truth of the UFO enigma, of the Roswell incident of 1947, and of what really goes down at Area 51. The Robertson Panel's conclusions, however, suggested that UFOs did not have a direct, significant impact on the United States' national security. Rather, the major worry of the panel was how the public mindset could, in theory, be affected by bogus tales of UFO encounters – and created and weaved by the Reds. On this very matter, the Robertson Panel recorded these words:

"Although evidence of any direct threat from these sightings was wholly lacking, related dangers might well exist resulting from: A. Misidentification of actual enemy artifacts by defense personnel. *B. Overloading of emergency reporting channels with 'false' information. C. Subjectivity of public to mass hysteria and greater vulnerability to possible enemy psychological warfare* [italics mine]."

Clearly, when it came to UFOs, it was those matters concerning "mass hysteria" and "false information" that dominated the thinking of the Robertson Panel. The possible presence of *real* aliens in the United States seemed to be very much in the background for the CIA. There was also a recommendation that a number of the public UFO investigative groups that existed in the United States at the time should be "watched" carefully due to "the apparent irresponsibility and the possible use of such groups for subversive purposes." For the CIA, "subversive purposes" meant the actions of the Soviets, or, worse, of home-grown-and-groomed communists. Maybe both. It's entirely possible that at least *some* reports of fear-filled encounters with the so-called "Men in Black" in that era may have been provoked by such surveillance. Particularly so if UFO researchers were threatened by fedora-sporting and trench-coat-wearing government agents late at night – which typifies the appearances and actions of the MIB. I should stress that not all of the Men in Black can be said to come from the government. As I note in my 2018 book, *The Black Diary*, and as incredible as it may sound, at least some of the Men in Black may have unearthly origins. Let's now address one example of how and why the CIA carefully watched UFO research groups in that era. An agency document of February 9, 1953 begins as follows:

1. Recently a member of the Los Angeles Office had occasion to hear Dr. Walter Riedel tell something of the activities of the California Committee for Saucer Investigations (CSI). His comments, as follows, may be of interest:

2. Dr. Riedel indicated he was formerly Chief Designer at the German Experimental Rocket Center at Peenemunde. He has been in the US as a "paperclip" scientist for some years. He is now a Project engineer in the Aerophysics Department (Guided Missiles) of the North American Aviation Corp. He gave every impression of being a competent scientist, especially knowledgeable on rocket matters. He seemed a balanced person, not given to fixations.

3. CSI has been in operation some years, composed of private individuals intrigued and scientifically interested in finding an explanation for "saucer" phenomena. To date, they have received some 1570 letters relating to reported sightings. Of this number, they have been able to immediately or quickly eliminate 75% as not worth follow-up. The great proportion of this 25% has been discarded upon further investigation. What was somewhat surprising to the writer was the exhaustiveness with which these investigations are being made. Not only are very careful calculations made, if the data exists, to check the possibility of the report being physically possible (e.g., in terms of lines of sight), but the individual reporting the sighting is investigated privately at his place of residence to establish a general background of reliability and credibility.

4. Of the 25% investigated, perhaps 25 or so sightings have been established as "reliable" in the sense that no known existing explanation exists for them. Apparently, most of these have been forwarded to Wright Field, Dayton, Ohio, although there appears to be a time lag of some duration while CSI is making its own check and calculations. Dr.

Riedel's description of one reported sighting by a TWA pilot and crew, and the follow-up with respect to it, was impressive to the writer in the thought applied, the pains taken, and the very careful application of scientific method. So serious is CSI with respect to its investigations that Dr. Riedel indicated that they are going to execute a planned "hoax" over the Los Angeles area, in order to test the reaction and reliability of the public in general to unusual aerial phenomena. (The sightings reported over Malibu in its Los Angeles papers of 30 Jan 53 could possibly be this hoax.) From this experiment, they hope to ascertain how many people report an aerial visual phenomenon which had been conducted so as to be clearly visible to a large number of people in the area. They will also, of course, be able to test the variation of report details, etc. This experiment is designed to give a better background against which future sightings can be evaluated."

5. *Apparently, an eye and interest are also directed toward the USSR for reactions to sightings as reported in the PRAVDA are observed* [italics mine]. This interest is also evident in the paper entitled "Rockets Behind the Iron Curtain," presented before the annual convention of the American Rocket Society in New York City on 4 December 1952, by George P. Sutton, also of Aerophysics Department (North American Aviation, Inc.) and associated with CSI.

6. Of incidental interest may be the fact that NAA (National Aeronautical Association) suggested politely and perhaps indirectly to Dr. Riedel that he disassociate himself from official membership on CSI."

Now, we get to the heart of the Robertson Panel's concerns: the Russian angle of it all. One of the panel's chief recommendations was for the creation of "a public education campaign" that should be undertaken on matters relative to UFOs. Specifically, agreed the members, such a program would...

...result in reduction in public interest in "flying saucers" which today evokes a strong psychological reaction. This education could be accomplished by mass media such as television, motion pictures, and popular articles. Basis of such education would be actual case histories that had been puzzling at first but later explained. As in the case of conjuring tricks, there is much less stimulation if the "secret" is known. Such a program should tend to reduce the current gullibility of the public and consequently their susceptibility to clever hostile propaganda.

In this connection, Dr. Hadley Cantril (Princeton University) was suggested. Cantril authored "*Invasion from Mars*," (a study in the psychology of panic, written about the famous Orson Welles radio broadcast in 1938) and has since performed advanced laboratory studies in the field of perception. The names of Don Marquis (University of Michigan) and Leo Roston were mentioned as possibly suitable as consultant psychologists.

Also, someone familiar with mass communications techniques, perhaps an advertising expert, would be helpful. Arthur Godfrey was mentioned as possibly a valuable channel of communication reaching a mass audience of certain levels. Dr. Berkner suggested the U. S. Navy (ONR) Special Devices Center, Sands Point, L. I., as a potentially valuable organization to assist in such an educational program. The teaching techniques used by this agency for aircraft identification during the past war [were] cited as an example of a similar educational task. The Jam Handy Company, which made World War II training films (motion picture and slide strips), was also suggested, as well as Walt Disney, Inc. animated cartoons.

We see that the Robertson Panel's recommendations were driven not by the presence of real extraterrestrials, but by a fear of "clever hostile propaganda." By now, you know only too well who the panel thought was behind such propaganda. David Goodman, at Oxford Scholarship Online, says the following of *The War of the Worlds* broadcast and Hadley Cantril: "Intense anxiety about propaganda on the radio in the late 1930s created a cultural and intellectual climate that placed the credulity and intelligence of the American population under scrutiny as never before. Aspects of the civic paradigm proved divisive in practice. The panicked listeners to the Mars broadcast were repeatedly and aggressively blamed for their failure as citizens to listen correctly; they in turn argued back that of course they expected truth from radio. Social psychologists such as Hadley Cantril were central to the interpretation of the panic, elaborating rather than abandoning public concerns about intelligence and civic capacity."

As for how the Walt Disney Corporation and Ward Kimball became a part of the equation, Robbie Graham, the author of *Silver Screen Saucers*, states: "The panel's singling-out of Disney made sense given the animation giant's then firmly established working relationship with the U.S. government: during World War II Disney made numerous propaganda shorts for the U.S. military, and in the 1950s corporate and government sponsors helped the company produce films promoting President Eisenhower's 'Atoms for Peace' policy, as well as the retrospectively hilarious *Duck and*

Cover documentary, which depicted schoolchildren surviving an atomic attack by sheltering under their desks."

Graham had more to say: "That the Robertson Panel highlighted Disney is significant in that the Panel's general recommendation to debunk UFOs through media channels is known to have been acted upon in at least one instance: this being the CBS TV broadcast of *UFOs: Friend, Foe, or Fantasy?* (1966), an anti-UFO documentary narrated by Walter Cronkite. In a letter addressed to former Robertson Panel Secretary Frederick C. Durant, Dr. Thornton Page confided that he 'helped organize the CBS TV show around the Robertson Panel conclusions,' even though this was thirteen years after the Panel had first convened. In light of this case alone, it seems reasonable to assume that the government may at least have attempted to follow through on the Robertson Panel's Disney recommendation."

Ward Kimball largely kept his and Disney's ties to the CIA and UFOs a secret until 1979. Perhaps the bodies of dead aliens really are hidden in a fortified, well-guarded bunker deep below the agency's headquarters in Langley, Virginia. Maybe, the CIA even has a crashed UFO stored away; the remains of the alleged extraterrestrial spacecraft said to have been found in the blisteringly hot wilds of New Mexico in the summer of 1947. Possibly, the CIA knows all about an alien presence on our planet. It has to be said, however, that the vast majority of the available data and documentation from the CIA that links the agency to flying saucers, does *not* revolve around real E.T.s. The truth of the matter is that it points in a very different direction. It's a direction that leads us to the realm of Russia-manufactured tales of E.T.s, created and used to try and frighten Americans in the early years of the Cold War.

Now, we come to a very strange aspect of the Robertson Panel story, one filled with mystery and intrigue. And Russians.

And a former communist who believed the Soviets were using UFO-driven psychological warfare tactics to destabilize people of the United States.

Nineteen-fifty-five was the year in which the late L. Ron Hubbard's Church of Scientology released a publication with an eye-opening title: *Brain-Washing: A Synthesis of the Russian Textbook on Psychopolitics*. It was said at the time that *Brain-Washing* was an overview of the activities of a man named Lavrentiy Beria. The Atomic Heritage Foundation says of Beria: "In 1938, Stalin summoned Beria to Moscow and appointed him as deputy to the chief of the Soviet secret police, the NKVD. Within the course of a couple years, Beria orchestrated the execution of NKVD chief Nikolai Yezhov and then assumed his predecessor's position."

Beria was executed, in December 1953, for treason.

It has been said that *Brain-Washing* was inspired by a lecture that Lavrentiy Beria gave at the dawning of the 1950s. The subject of that same lecture was the ways and means by which psychiatry could control the mindset of significant numbers of people. L. Ron Hubbard, Jr. has gone on the record as saying of *Brain-Washing*: "Dad wrote every word of it. Barbara Bryan [an assistant to Hubbard] and my wife typed the manuscript off his dictation."

It's eye-opening to note that the introduction to one particular version of *Brain-Washing* was written by a man named Kenneth Goff (several versions are in circulation and have been for years). It just so happens that Wisconsin-born Goff was a former communist who spent much of the 1950s and 1960s warning people of the threat that the Russians posed to the United States. Notably, Goff – whose FBI file is *huge* - believed that the Soviet Union was using the UFO subject as a means to exert control over the West. One of Goff's lectures was titled "Traitors in the Pulpit, or

What's Behind the Flying Saucers – Are they from Russia, Another Planet, or God?" In his 1959 booklet, *Red Shadows*, Goff wrote the following words:

> "During the past few years, the flying saucer scare has rapidly become one of the main issues, used by organizations working for a one-world government, to frighten people into the belief that we will need a super world government to cope with an invasion from another planet. Many means are being used to create a vast amount of imagination in the minds of the general public, concerning the possibilities of an invasion by strange creatures from Mars or Venus. This drive began early in the 40's, with a radio drama, put on my Orson Welles, which caused panic in many of the larger cities of the East, and resulted in the death of several people. The Orson Welles program of invasion from Mars was used by the Communist Party as a test to find out how the people would react on instructions given out over the radio. It was an important part of the Communist rehearsal for the Revolution."

You will recall that the Orson Welles production of H.G. Wells' *The War of the Worlds* is referenced in the pages of the Robertson Panel report. In some respects, Goff's concerns and worries mirrored those of the Robertson Panel. This is made all the more significant by the fact that, in his communist days, Goff had connections to a long-forgotten UFO researcher of the early 1950s. That man was Karl Hunrath, who vanished under very mysterious circumstances in November 1953, along with a colleague in UFO research, Wilbur Wilkinson. They did so after taking to the skies from a California airport. Neither man was ever seen again. Like Goff, a Wisconsin native, Hunrath, in the early 1950s, was suspected of being in league with the Russians. It was a story that Goff shared with the FBI, and which Contactee George Hunt Wiliamson confirmed hearing from Al Bailey, of George Adamski's circle. A file was opened on Hunrath by the FBI, chiefly because, in 1953, he claimed to have developed a strange contraption – to which, oddly, he gave the name "Bosco" – that could bring down American military planes.

There are also rumors that, as a Soviet asset, Hunrath was ordered by his Kremlin masters to try and penetrate the heart of the Robertson Panel. Incredibly, there is a small body of data in support of this claim. According to the legendary cartoonist R. Crumb, on one occasion while visiting his good friend - and Robertson Panel asset - Ward Kimball, and with fellow artists Bob Armstrong and Al Dodge, Kimball "…told us an interesting story. Back in the 1950s they were working on a series about rockets and outer space technology for the Disneyland TV show. I remember seeing those shows when I was a kid. There was a scientist named Wilkins who worked on the project. Wilkins started bringing around this guy called 'Huunrath', supposedly a colleague of his. Kimball said at first no one took much notice of the guy Huunrath. He was just unobtrusive. He was kind of strange. He didn't say much. He walked kind of stiffly and he wore a suit and tie that were ill-fitting."

Crumb was slightly erroneous in terms of the names. It's clear that "Wilkins" and "Huunrath" were really Wilkinson and Hunrath. The Hunrath-Kimball-Wilkinson meetings can only have occurred in 1953, as the pair vanished forever in November of that year. That Hunrath was getting close to Ward Kimball - who was already on-board with the CIA's Robertson Panel - demonstrated Hunrath's determination to uncover the scoop on what was afoot at a deep, official level regarding the Robertson Panel, UFOs and the U.S. Government. And to hand over that same scoop to his Russian handlers, no less.

9.

"A POSSIBLE COMMUNIST MENACE TO SAUCER ENTHUSIASTS"

One of those who, in the 1950s, took a deep interest in the Russian connection to the flying saucer phenomenon was the late Jim Moseley, who died in 2012 at the age of eighty-one, and whose opinions on George Adamski we have already digested. For the ufologically-minded, Moseley was without a doubt most associated with his highly entertaining newsletter, *Saucer Smear*. It was a semi-regular, self-published collection of Moseley's comments, rants and observations on the UFO research scene. Moseley was someone who, in later years, focused just about all of his time and effort on poking fun at ufologists whenever and wherever he could. He did so in a very witty fashion, too. I should stress, though, that Moseley did have a real, deep interest in the UFO phenomenon itself. And a firm belief in it, too. Right up until the time of his death.

Back in 1953 Moseley hit the road – in what really *was* a definitive Jack Kerouac/Neal Cassady-style – in search of the answers to what was going on in the heavens above. What Moseley found out, as he traveled from New York to California and back again, was a significantly varied and entertaining collection of eccentrics, liars, nut-jobs, and – to Moseley's relief - genuinely interesting eyewitnesses to strange, aerial craft in the skies of 1950s America. Altogether, Moseley interviewed around one hundred people, on a clunky big recorder, which was no mean feat. The list of interviewees included George Adamski himself and Frank Scully, the man whose 1950 book, *Behind the Flying Saucers*, led to Silas Newton's secret recruitment by agents of the U.S. government, as revealed by the CIA's Karl Pflock.

Moseley's coast-to-coast trip was funded by a guy named Ken Krippine. He was a somewhat shady, dubious character who had suggested that if he, Moseley, would do all of the research, then Krippine would write a book on Moseley's UFO findings. The two would then split the profits right down the middle. Sounds good, right? Well, for a while, yes, it sounded *very* good. The proposed book, however, did not materialize; at least not as Moseley and Krippine had originally planned things. No, it wasn't due to the infernal intervention of the mysterious Men in Black. Rather, it was all due to a distinct lack of interest on the part of just about every publisher that Moseley approached with his well-thumbed and increasingly-creased and crumpled manuscript. Moseley was not one to be daunted, however. Years later – decades, in fact – he put just about all of his old notes and audio-recordings to good use in his hilarious autobiography, *Shockingly Close to the Truth*, which was written with Karl Pflock.

It was in 1955 that Moseley, in his own words, "had fallen under the influence" of a man named Charles Samwick. The latter was someone who, before retiring from the U.S. Army, worked in the hall-and-mirrors-filled world of counter-intelligence, which included keeping a very close eye on what the Russians were said to be up to *inside* the United States. Not only that, Moseley was able to determine that Samwick had, in some hazy, unclear fashion, ties to the CIA's Robertson Panel and had once helped to bust a Soviet spy-ring in Washington, D.C. Samwick and Moseley soon became good buddies, with Moseley somewhat dazzled and disturbed by one particular thing Samwick had to say. He told Moseley: "The Communist Party has planted an agent in every civilian saucer club in the United States." Whether this was true, or amounted to hard-to-prove words inspired by the likes of Joseph McCarthy, Moseley was in no position to disagree with his well-informed source. But, he did make Samwick's revelations the subject of an editorial in his pre-*Saucer Smear* newsletter, *Saucer News*. In the June-July 1955 issue Moseley revealed the following to his eager readers, but specifically without revealing Samwick's name:

> Although it is perhaps unwise to inject a political note into a flying saucer magazine, we feel obliged to point out to our readers certain dangers which, taken together, add up to a possible Communist menace to saucer enthusiasts. First, for several months we have had good reason to believe that Communist agents have been planted in all of America's leading saucer groups, for information-gathering purposes. This in itself is not a startling fact, but it should serve as a note of caution to saucer researchers who in the course of their studies might unearth information of a technical military nature.
>
> Secondly, let us all give some very serious consideration to the many alleged space men being called to the public's attention – all of whom invariably tell us of the dangers of war and the exploitation of atomic energy. No one desires peace any more than we do, but let us remember too that it is part of the Communist "peace line" to frighten the American people into ceasing our atomic experiments. It is quite possible that some of these 'space men' are unwittingly playing into the hands of the Communists.
>
> Last, but not least, let us not fall into the pitfall of condemning the Government of the United States just

because the Air Force refuses to tell us all we would like to know about flying saucers – I have been told that some of the remarks made at the Saucer Convention last March came dangerously close to sedition!

Even as ardently loyal saucer fans, we all can and should face the fact that there are more important and immediate problems in the world today. Whether the saucers are held to be from Space or Earth, it is quite obvious that they present no immediate threat to the safety of this Country; so there is nothing to worry about. Of course everyone would be happier if "officialdom" would be more generous with its information on saucers, but for the present we can only assume that there is a good sufficient reason for the continuing scarcity of information from official sources.

In making the above remarks, we are *not* referring to any particular individual or organization in the field of saucer research. We are merely observing that the saucerian field is alarmingly ripe for use in furthering Communist ends. Let each individual among us be on his guard that he does not fall into such a trap.

Now, let's focus on Truman Bethurum. He was a contactee who had a decade or so of fame in the arena of the Space Brothers. His 1954 book, *Aboard a Flying Saucer*, remains a Contactee classic of its kind. Jim Moseley got to know Bethurum well. In the 1950s, Bethurum claimed flirty, late-night close encounters with a beautiful alien space-babe named Aura Rhanes. "Tops in shapeliness and beauty" was the way Bethurum described "the captain" of the ship. The locations of all the action were almost always isolated areas of Nevada's expansive Mormon Mountains. Most ufologists of the day, very understandably, dismissed Bethurum's tales as fantasies run wild and free. It's intriguing, however, to note the following words from Bethurum:

"Two or three fellows who had sons in Korea and who read a lot in the newspapers about the Communist underground in this country, were convinced in their own minds that I was, if making contact with anyone at all, *making it with enemy agents* [italics mine]. They even went so far as to tell me belligerently that they intended to get guns and follow me nights, and if they caught up me having intercourse with any people from planes, airships of any kind, they'd blast me and those people too."

Was Aura Rhanes a figment of Bethurum's imagination? Could she have been an alien? Might she have been one of those "enemy agents" to which Bethurum referred? A Russian plant seeking to manipulate the UFO scene? Taking into consideration all that we have learned so far, we should not dismiss the latter possibility out of hand. On a related matter, it's worth noting that FBI records demonstrate that in December 1954, the Palm Springs Republican Club contacted the FBI to inquire if Bethurum might be guilty of "trying to put over any propaganda."

Bethurum, not surprisingly, became the subject of an FBI file that ran to a couple of dozen pages. It was primarily focused on those "enemy agent"-driven comments that Bethurum himself highlighted on the lecture circuit. Once again we see evidence of government concerns about a contactee, propaganda, and possible foreign operatives – and all in relation to controversial tales of aliens. Also in 1954, the FBI sat up and took notice when Bethurum announced plans to speak at an event in Ohio with fellow contactee, George Hunt Williamson. As we've seen, Williamson was hardly unknown to the FBI.

10.

"A SUBVERSIVE ELEMENT"

Did U.S. agents, in the 1950s, clandestinely drug one of the early Contactees, specifically as a means to determine if he was working with the Soviets to promote communism? It's a loaded question that takes us down some dark and winding alleyways, to say the least. The story – worthy of a Hollywood movie of conspiratorial proportions – is one of those too good to be true sagas that, incredibly, turned out to be true, after all. The poor figure who found himself caught in a state of fear and paranoia was Orfeo Angelucci; he was a somewhat meek, fragile character who was blighted by ill-health and low-esteem from childhood. That is, until he had a series of life-changing UFO encounters that energized him and gave him a new lease on life. It's fair to say that Angelucci was someone who very much rode on the coattails of the likes of Georges one, two and three: that's Adamski, Van Tassel, and Williamson. Angelucci never reached the stratospheric heights of Adamski. He was, though, one of the key players in the Contactee arena of the 1950s. Little did Angelucci realize that he would one day attract the attention of government agents and the military; they were determined to uncover the truth of the man's claims and connections, by fair means or foul. Mostly foul, as it turned out.

In April 1952, Angelucci secured a good job with the Lockheed Aircraft Corporation in Burbank, California, specifically in the

Plastics Unit. On May 23, 1952 Angelucci was working the late-shift at Lockheed. It wasn't long after midnight when he finally hit the road, looking forward to seeing his wife. All was normal. That is, until it wasn't. While he drove along Los Angeles' Victory Boulevard things became strange; *very* strange. Out of the corner of his eye, Angelucci saw a bright, red light; it was moving low in the dark skies. Puzzled, he slowed down his car and kept his eye on the whatever-it-was. It didn't appear to be a solid, nuts-and-bolts aircraft of some sort. Rather, it was a ball of light, around five times the size of an average traffic light. Somewhat disturbingly, and as Angelucci continued his drive, the light appeared to be shadowing him. Feeling nervous, he decided to keep driving and hoped that the light would vanish. It did not. Shortly after crossing a bridge over the Los Angeles River, and at an intersection which Angelucci described as a "lonely, deserted stretch of road called Forest Lawn Drive," a pair of small lights – maybe around two feet in diameter – shot out of the larger light, which soared into the dark skies. Angelucci brought his car to the proverbial screeching halt. He could only sit and stare as the pair of lights bobbed in the air, like floating beach balls. Suddenly, there was a development; an astounding one.

As Angelucci looked on, a voice emanated from one of the balls. According to the man himself, it was "a masculine voice in strong, well-modulated tones and speaking perfect English." The voice assured Angelucci that he should not afraid; no harm would come to him. Stressing to Angelucci that he was in the company of friends, the voice said, in a typical, know-it-all Space Brother fashion: "Man believes himself civilized, but often his thoughts are barbaric and his emotions lethal. We do not say this as criticism, but state it only as fact. Thus it is best to approach all planetary visitors with friendly, welcoming thoughts."

The lights shot away, leaving Angelucci amazed and excited. Two months later, he would have yet another encounter.

It was the night of July 23, 1952 and Angelucci felt compelled to head out to the Glendale Hyperion Bridge, which crosses the Los Angeles River and Interstate 5. He did so on foot. In his own words, "dense, oblique shadows down below" transformed things into "a shadowed no-man's land." His breathing became shallow, his hands and legs tingled, and a rising panic-attack threatened to overwhelm him. Then, suddenly, a "huge, misty soap bubble squatting on the ground, emitting a fuzzy pale glow" appeared before him. That soap bubble-type light suddenly transformed into what appeared to be a solid metallic craft. Angelucci moved slowly towards it; entering the object through a small doorway and into a darkened room. It contained nothing but a chair. On sitting down, Angelucci soon felt unable to move; his body was suddenly weak and heavy. It was, he claimed, all due to the effects of G-forces: the craft was apparently high in the sky in no time at all. Peering out of a conveniently positioned window, Angelucci could see the bright lights of Los Angeles glowing far below him. The lights got fainter and fainter as the craft got progressively higher and higher: "I trembled as I realized I was actually looking upon a planet from somewhere out in space."

A booming voice suddenly filled the room: "Orfeo, you are looking upon Earth – your home! From here, over a thousand miles away, in space, it appears as the most beautiful planet in the heavens and a haven of peace and tranquility. But you and your Earthly brothers know the true conditions there." He was warned that an "hour of crisis" was looming; that the human race was in a state of major uncertainty that just might lead to a disastrous atomic war between East and West. Instantly, and as the Lord's Prayer boomed out of unseen speakers, Angelucci knew he had to do the bidding of the invisible entities on-board the spaceship: spread the word of friendly aliens from a faraway world. In minutes, he was returned to the shadow-filled bridge and left to make his way home. Angelucci's life – which was to be filled with further encounters of the peace and love type - would never be quite the same again.

Like so many of the Contactees, Angelucci was soon on the lecture circuit, which included becoming a regular at George Van Tassel's gigs out at Giant Rock, California. Angelucci also turned his attention to writing books; his most remembered one being 1955's *The Secret of the Saucers*. Now, it's time to get to the second part of the Angelucci story. It's one that revolves around not aliens, but the military: "secret-agents" and one of the most notorious periods in the history of the CIA.

By the mid-1950s, Angelucci had moved on from his job at Lockheed and he and his family were now based out of Twentynine Palms, San Bernadino County, California. And, with *The Secret of the Saucers* on the bookshelves, he was becoming a familiar face at UFO lectures and conferences. It was in this period that Angelucci caught the attention of the FBI – and for a very curious reason. As he became more adept at public speaking, and more comfortable about discussing his claimed encounters with aliens, Angelucci revealed something disturbingly eye-opening. It was something that soon had the Feds on his tail. According to Angelucci, as his profile as one of the Contactees grew and grew, he found himself approached on several occasions by what he described as a "subversive element." This small group – "foreigners," as he worded it - first approached Angelucci while he was engaged in a series of lectures along the east coast in the 1950s. Regular UFO enthusiasts, they were certainly not. They did their very best to try and encourage Angelucci to suggest to his listeners and readers that his alien comrades were communists. In correspondence with Jim Moseley, who, as we have seen, spent time addressing the matter of a Russian plot to manipulate the U.S. UFO scene,

Angelucci claimed that this "gang of four," as we might describe them, bought him dinner on three occasions and plied him with plentiful amounts of booze in plush New York hotels and bars.

Angelucci admitted to Moseley that he was "flattered" by the attention, but remained very uneasy about the agenda. Angelucci would later say of this curious affair: "Failing in their desperate attempts to convert me to communism and slant my talks along the Party Line, they invariably defiantly demanded: 'Well, then, just what do you think is wrong with Communism?'"

Shortly before Angelucci publicly revealed that a certain "subversive element" was mixing and stirring left-wing, extremist politics with extraterrestrials, the FBI came knocking on the front-door of the Angelucci home. While we don't know the full story, we do at least have the bones of it, thanks to Jim Moseley. According to what Angelucci told Moseley, a pair of FBI agents visited Angelucci at his Twentynine Palms home, telling him that they had heard of the actions of this East Coast group – from who, though, was something that the FBI was not prepared to reveal. The questions posed to Angelucci were many: How did he first meet the group? Did they give their names? Were they Americans? Did they offer him money to slant his tales down a politically-driven path? The list of questions went on and on.

Angelucci – admittedly scared out of his wits by the fact that the FBI was onto him, even though he hadn't really done anything wrong – blurted out just about all that he could. The group had first approached him, in an overly friendly fashion, at a lecture in New York, he told the special-agents. No names were ever given to him, but all four were well-dressed, all seemed to be around the forty-mark, and all had overseas accents. No money ever crossed hands. They invited Angelucci to dinner, which he accepted, admittedly intrigued by the prospect of developing new contacts. It was over dinner that the matter of communism surfaced its head.

Angelucci, knowing it was useless to try and deceive the FBI, admitted to the G-Men that he listened to what the group had to say about those mysterious characters with a supposed love of communism, but made it very clear that he had no time for the Russians and their way of life. The tone then became noticeably disturbing, with a suggestion from the mysterious men that things just might become extremely difficult for Angelucci if he didn't go along with their plans. Angelucci told Moseley that he never really knew what that meant, only that it "upset me" and he quickly left. Angelucci further told the FBI that the same group attended a lecture he gave – also on the East Coast – a week or so later. Once again, the conversation began cordially, but certainly did not remain that way: it was filled with threats and worrying innuendo. The four, seemingly by now extremely frustrated by Angelucci's stubborn stance on politics, abruptly vanished into the night leaving him decidedly shaken and stirred.

Incredibly, and as time went on, Angelucci wondered if the mysterious group were aliens themselves, human-like beings visiting the Earth from a world faraway and with a communist-like government. Had Angelucci chose to step back for a moment, taken a deep breath, and cleared his head, he just might have come to the conclusion that his strange visitors were really from right here on Earth. But not from the United States. You know from where.

The third and final meeting with these strange figures occurred in 1956, at a lecture given by Angelucci in Los Angeles. He told the story of his 1952 encounters, received significant applause, and signed a few books for eager fans. And there was that same group, too: looming and lurking, speaking to many of the attendees, and keeping distinctly eagle-eyes on Angelucci. As the night came to an end, once again they made an attempt to bring Angelucci into their fold. But, to his credit, he was having none of it. Interestingly, one of the men, who Angelucci described to Moseley as "the boss," told Angelucci that should he, Angelucci, change his mind, he could contact them by calling the manager of Cincinnati, Ohio's Sheraton Gibson Hotel. Angelucci chose not to. And, in essence, that was the story he told to the FBI.

The two FBI agents thanked Angelucci, assured him that he was not in any kind of trouble (he was clearly an innocent pawn in a far bigger picture) and left. We do not know how, or even if, things proceeded further with regard to the FBI, Angelucci, and that certain hotel in Ohio. There is a very good and *potentially* mysterious reason for that: on October 24, 2017, the FBI informed UFO researcher John Greenewald that Angelucci had indeed been the subject of a Bureau file, but that it was destroyed on October 30, 2009.

Evidently, the meeting with the FBI shook Angelucci severely; in fact, so severely he decided to release the following statement, probably to ensure that the FBI fully understood that he was not someone with communist leanings: "Communism is the negation of all that is honest and good in the world and in humanity. They would enslave the human mind. Their obstructiveness is willful and planned. We must eventually meet this murderous element at Armageddon; when it will be victory for one side or the other. Good will triumph, or evil! Every entity in the world and the adjoining planes is now aligned definitely upon one side or the other. No matter what the outcome of the conflict, the positive element of good will ultimately attain a greater life and progression; whereas the negative will meet death, destruction and a new beginning in a more hostile environment. As you have made your choice, so be it!"

There is an interesting, additional piece of data that deserves to be shared: In 1954, a group of West Coast-based Contactees – including Truman Bethurum and George Hunt Williamson – gave a series of lectures in Cincinnati. As this was also the home-city of famed UFO researcher Leonard Stringfield, paths inevitably crossed. Hoping to get Stringfield to endorse their talks, Bethurum, Williamson and their flock called at his home and introduced themselves. Stringfield flatly refused to lend his support; although he did invite the group into his home. It was while in the company of the Contactees that Stringfield had an intriguing experience, as he noted in his 1977 book, *Situation Red: The UFO Siege*:

"After their departure I began to wonder about their causes. At one point during the evening's many tête-à-têtes, I chanced to overhear two members discussing the FBI. Pretending aloofness, I tried to overhear more. It seemed that one person was puzzling over the presence of an 'agent' in the group. When I was caught standing too close, the FBI talk stopped. Whether or not I had reason to be suspicious, it was not difficult for me to believe that some of the Contactees behind all this costly showmanship were official 'plants.'" Planted by the Russians? We shouldn't ignore such a possibility.

Interestingly, the lectures in question were held at the Sheraton Gibson Hotel, two years before Angelucci was told that his communist sources could be contacted at that very same hotel. Was it once the temporary "home" of a group of Soviet agents? Or of Russia-loving Americans brought into a weird program to manipulate the world of Ufology? Answers elude us. The hotel was demolished in 1977, its staff of the 1950s are likely all dead now, and, as we've seen, any and all FBI documentation on Angelucci was relegated to the shredder or the furnace around a decade after this book was published. But it's not quite "case closed."

We now come to the finale. And what a finale it really is.

It wasn't just the FBI keeping watch on Orfeo Angelucci; fears he may have been in cahoots with Soviet agents or assets circulated. Others within the government were doing likewise, too. In correspondence with Jim Moseley, Angelucci said he that had previously been visited – back in 1954, and a year before the FBI began looking into his activities in fifty-five – by what he termed "Army boys." They were interested in his claims of alien contact, which, at the time, were largely not in the public domain (it was to be around another year before *The Secrets of the Saucers* surfaced), but which Angelucci had discussed with many while attending a California-based UFO convention. Critically, and at that same convention, Angelucci loudly discussed his thoughts on the issue of extraterrestrial politics. Unfortunately, Angelucci did not expand on what he meant by this to Moseley, but it may well have led government plants in the audience to make a decision to keep an eye on Angelucci – and to find what they could on matters relative to his relationship to politics and flying saucers. Such a thing is not at all impossible. For example, the FBI's declassified files on yet another of the early Contactees - one George Van Tassel, who put on yearly events out at Giant Rock, California - reveal that Bureau agents regularly attended Van Tassel's presentations, incognito of course.

On one particular night in December 1954, and while still working in Twentynine Palms, California, Angelucci headed out to a local eatery. That's where things got strange. Angelucci recorded: "I felt a strangeness in the air. There is a cosmic spell over the desert most of the time, but tonight the mystery was less distant and intangible; it was close and pulsating."

Angelucci was soon deep in conversation with a man who identified himself only as "Adam," a customer who claimed to be thirty-something and suffering from a terminal illness. Death was said to be just around the corner for the man. In an odd and synchronistic fashion, Adam claimed that he had read Angelucci's book, *The Secret of the Saucers*, that he considered their meeting to be beyond just an amazing coincidence, and that he wished to share his thoughts with Angelucci before time ran out. As in quite literally. But, said Adam, before their conversation could begin, Angelucci had to swallow a pill; of what kind Angelucci didn't know. That didn't stop him from doing exactly what Adam demanded from him, though. Angelucci took a gulp of water and the "oyster-white pellet" went down. For Angelucci, there was now no turning back. It didn't take long before he felt weird, odd, and out of this world. Spaced out. Fucked up. In short, Angelucci had been drugged. It was almost like one of the most famous scenes in the 1999 movie, *The Matrix*, starring Keanu Reeves. But this was the world of the real, not of Hollywood.

Angelucci said: "…I took the pellet and dropped it into my glass. Immediately the water bubbled, turning slowly into the clear, pale amber contained in [Adam's] own glass. I lifted the glass a few inches from the table, looking into it with a feeling that this might be the drink I dared not hope for. The exhilarating aroma rising from it could not be mistaken…I thrilled from head to foot as I took the glass, lifted it to my lips, and swallowed twice from it. At that instant, I entered, with Adam, into a more exalted state and everything around me took on a different semblance. No longer was I in Tiny's café in Twentynine Palms. It had been transformed into a cozy retreat on some radiant star system. Though everything remained in its same position, added beauty and meaning were given to the things and people present there.

"…*Among the patrons dining that evening were two marines from the nearby base. Sometimes they glanced our way as they talked and drank beer following their meal* [italics mine].

Angelucci said that Adam seemed oddly obsessed with the glass and was "fraught with expectancy." Suddenly, the sounds of music filled Angelucci's ears. Incredibly, the music seemed to be coming from the glass itself. Or, rather, that's how it seemed to Angelucci. The reality is that he was now stoned to a significant degree. Angelucci stared at the glass and saw the figure of "a miniature young woman" who was dancing in that same glass! That's right: the drugs were now kicking in to a serious degree. Of the small woman, Angelucci said, "her golden-blond beauty was as arresting as the miracle of her projection in the glass. Her arms moved in rhythmic motion with the graceful thrusts of her dancing body."

What began as a pleasant meeting between like-minded souls soon became a drug-driven interrogation. By Angelucci's own admission, he spilled the entire beans to Adam: the nature of his encounters, and the words of his alien friends. There was even a debate on politics, which is rather telling. Angelucci staggered home, his mind hardly his own for the next few hours.

When it comes to the matter of this suspicious saga, it's important to note the timeframe: the Cold War era. This was the period when research into "mind-control" was at its height. Over the course of several decades, the United States' intelligence community, military and government established and sponsored a number of programs relative to mind-control; many of those programs were focused on creating chemical cocktails designed to interrogate Soviet agents. The most notorious of the lot was Project MK-Ultra. It was a top-secret project overseen by the CIA's Office of Scientific Intelligence, and which had its origins in the Cold War era of the late 1940s and very early 1950s. To demonstrate the level of secrecy that surrounded Project MK-Ultra, even though it had kicked off years before, its existence was largely unknown outside of the intelligence world until 1975. That was when the Church Committee and the Rockefeller Commission finally began making their own investigations of the CIA's mind-control-related activities. The story that unfolded would prove to be both dark and disturbing. The scope of the project was spelled out in an August 1977 document titled *The Senate MK-Ultra Hearings* that was prepared by the Senate Select Committee on Intelligence and the Committee on Human Resources.

The author of the document provided these words:

"Research and development programs to find materials which could be used to alter human behavior were initiated in the late 1940s and early 1950s. These experimental programs originally included testing of drugs involving witting human subjects, and culminated in tests using unwitting, non-volunteer human subjects. These tests were designed to determine the potential effects of chemical or biological agents when used operationally against individuals unaware that they had received a drug."

Was Angelucci drugged by someone posing as a likeminded friend, but who, in reality, was a ruthless figure seeking answers to what was motivating Angelucci to get involved in the controversial fields of the Contactee and alien politics? A case can certainly be made that this is *exactly* what happened. We have Adam, the mysterious man who wished to learn more of Angelucci's thoughts on matters flying and saucer-shaped. Adam made sure that Angelucci took the mind-bending pill *before* matters began in earnest. And, we have a pair of marines sitting close by and "intently" watching the whole process – possibly ready to intervene if Angelucci had an adverse reaction to whatever it was he had knocked back.

We can argue endlessly over whether Orfeo Angelucci was indeed subjected to mind-altering substances or wasn't. It's important to note, however, that accounts like his don't stand alone. In fact, there are more than a few almost identical ones to choose from – and from the very same time as well. As an example of just one of many, I'll focus on the story of a man named Stanley Glickman. Salon.com notes: "Until his death in 1992, Glickman insisted that a CIA agent, who for 40 years he consistently described as having a clubfoot, had slipped him a mind-bending mickey in a glass of Chartreuse liqueur at a bar in Paris in 1952, driving Glickman mad and destroying his life."

The story of Glickman is, ultimately, a tragic and turbulent one. At the time of his strange encounter, Glickman, an American, was living and working in Paris, France. He was in his mid-twenties and life was good: he spent time at the Academie de la Grande Chaumiere and got to hang out with modernist painter and sculptor, Fernand Leger. Then, one night, things changed. In the latter part of 1952, Glickman met with a friend in the Paris-based *Cafe Select*. It was while the pair was hanging out and drinking coffee that something very weird happened. Two American men came into the cafe and soon engaged Glickman in a deep debate. Hank Albarelli's 2009 book, *A Terrible Mistake*, chronicles the history of MK-Ultra in detailed fashion and addresses the Glickman affair. Albarelli notes that "the two strangers fell into a heated debate with Glickman about *politics, power, and patriotism* [italics mine]."

The confrontational debate finally came to an end, at which point the two men offered Glickman a drink. Unwisely, he accepted it. Just as Angelucci did. As history has shown, it was just about the worst move that Glickman could have ever made. He soon found himself plunged into the hearts of a psychedelic nightmare. Glickman felt as if he was floating above the table. His perceptions, said Albarelli, "became distorted." The mysterious men watched on "intently," as Glickman's hallucinations became evermore graphic and terrifying. The odd pair soon thereafter exited the café. It was a situation that affected Glickman's whole life from thereon: delusions and a sense of going insane gripped him for weeks after he was hit by the mind-bending cocktail. Glickman was finally given shock-treatment at the American Hospital of Paris, but he was never quite the same again. Glickman gave up painting, moved back to the United States (New York), and ran an antiques shop for the rest of his life.

Notably, Glickman stated that one of the two men who engaged him had a very noticeable limp. This has given rise to the genuinely intriguing theory that the limping man was one Sydney Gottlieb. He was a chemist, and one of the key figures in the CIA's "mind-control" program, MK-Ultra. Gottlieb just happened to have a clubfoot. In Gottlieb's 1999 obituary, the U.K.'s *Independent* newspaper stated: "Gottlieb's contribution was to oversee MKUltra. From the early 1950s through most of the 1960s hundreds of American citizens were administered mind-altering drugs. One mental patient in Kentucky was given LSD for 174 consecutive days. In all the agency conducted 149 mind-control experiments. At least one 'participant' died as a result of the experiments and several others went mad."

The Alliance for Human Research Protection states that, in 1977, Glickman "...learned about Gottlieb and CIA's LSD experiments on unwitting involuntary subjects from the Kennedy congressional hearings. Glickman sued in 1981, but the trial was delayed 17 years on technical grounds, by which time Glickman had died in 1992."

There are undeniable parallels between the story of Orfeo Angelucci and the sad saga of Stanley Glickman. Both were dosed in cafes/diners. Both incidents occurred in the 1950s. Glickman's two characters debated him on his politics. Angelucci, in a curious way, had a tie to communism. And both Glickman and Angelucci were watched "intently," a word which both Angelucci and Albarelli used when telling their respective stories. All of which strongly suggests that, despite the known portions of the incredible story of Orfeo Angelucci and a mysterious group of communists, there may very well be far more to it than we will ever know. The government most definitely knows how to bury its secrets. It certainly did that when it came to the official – ultimately shredded – FBI dossier on Angelucci.

Senator Joseph McCarthy (Wikimedia Commons)

The site of the mysterious Roswell affair of 1947.
Russian origins? (Nick Redfern)

Karl Pflock and UFOs: "Some sort of psychological warfare operation" (Nick Redfern)

PLANT

. An abandoned silvery disc was found in the deep rock-coal seams in Norwegian coal mines on Spitzbergen. It was pierced and marked by micrometeor impacts and bore all traces of having performed a long space voyage. It was sent for analysis to the Pentagon and disappeared there.

Nothing but a saucer put out of commission a high-voltage power transmission line in 1965 and thus plunged several large American cities into darkness for six hours.

A National Security Agency document refers to the Spitsbergen UFO crash of 1952 as a "Plant" (National Security Agency)

From magic to the military: Jasper Maskelyne, far right (Wikimedia Commons)

Beware of the Flatwoods Monster (Denise Rector)

The Aetherius Society: "It crusades for the suspension of the H-bomb tests" (Nick Redfern)

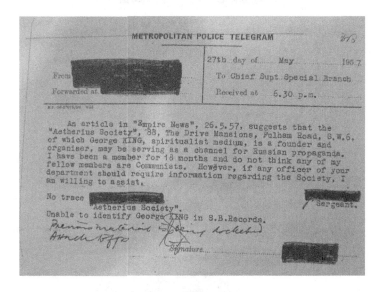

An extract from the Special Branch files on the Aetherius Society (Special Branch)

Lavrentiy Pavlovich Beria, the People's Commissar for Internal Affairs of the USSR (Wikimedia Commons)

Ben Chifley, Prime Minister of Australia from 1945 to 1949 (National Library of Australia)

In the early 1960s, U.S. intelligence planned to fake a
second coming of Jesus in the skies over Cuba. The purpose:
to overthrow Fidel Castro (Library of Congress)

Alice Bradley Sheldon, pictured with her husband, Huntington. Alice wrote alien-themed sci-fi and worked for the CIA (Chicago Tribune, January 24, 1946)

Greg Bishop at the grave of Paul Bennewitz (Nick Redfern)

Nikola Tesla, who is referenced in the most recently surfaced
Majestic 12 papers (Wikimedia Commons)

11.

"IT CRUSADES FOR THE SUSPENSION OF THE H-BOMB TESTS"

"The Aetherius Society is an international spiritual organization dedicated to spreading, and acting upon, the teachings of advanced extraterrestrial intelligences," its members state. They continue: "In great compassion, these beings recognize the extent of suffering on Earth and have made countless sacrifices in their mission to help us to create a better world. The Society was founded in the mid-1950s by an Englishman named George King shortly after he was contacted in London by an extraterrestrial intelligence known as 'Aetherius.' The main body of the Society's teachings consists of the wisdom given through the mediumship of Dr. King by the Master Aetherius and other advanced intelligences from this world and beyond. The single greatest aspect of the Society's teachings is the importance of selfless service to others."

UFO researchers David Clarke and Andy Roberts say: "The Aetherius Society were never a huge organization, indeed their numbers rarely totaled more than one thousand members worldwide...The Aetherius Society was not for everyone but, for those seekers who wanted or needed a spiritual dimension to their saucer beliefs, they provided a philosophy, structure and network of sincere like-minded souls."

George King suffered a heart-attack in 1986, underwent a multiple heart bypass in 1992, and died in Santa Barbara on July 12, 1997. The Aetherius Society, though, continues to thrive. Now, it's time to address matters relative to the Aetherius Society, nuclear weapons, Russia, the U.K.'s Communist Party, and the secret surveillance of ufologists.

So far as can be determined, George King and his Aetherius Society did not attract the secret attention of the world of officialdom until 1957, specifically in May of that year. It was on the 26th of the month that an eye-catching article appeared in the pages of a weekly U.K.-based publication called *The Empire News*. In an article titled "Flying Saucer Clubs Probe: Peace Messages 'from outer space,'" the following was revealed: "'Warnings' from outer space against Britain's H-Bomb tests published in a flying saucer magazine take a similar line to Moscow-inspired propaganda. The 'warning' – in a special issue of the magazine – is being scrutinized by Scotland Yard's Special Branch [the origins of which date back to 1883 and which, in 2006, was absorbed into the Metropolitan Police Service's Counter Terrorism Command]. It is suspected that a number of flying saucer clubs – and some spiritualists as well – are unwittingly being used by the communists. The warning appears in the magazine of the Aetherius Society, which circulates widely among flying saucer enthusiasts."

Not only that, *The Empire News* revealed that George King had, as he put it, received a channeled message from advanced entities from the planet Mars. Its decidedly anti-nuke message went as follows: "Have not the latest peace moves come from Russia? You in the West blame Russia and say it is necessary to make these weapons to protect yourselves from them. You in Britain are in a favorable position to show the larger countries the way."

It's hardly surprising that a body like Special Branch would sit up and take notice of (a) this development in the world of the Aetherius Society and (b) the pro-Russian words of the Martians. King wasted no time in contacting Scotland Yard, demanding to know why, exactly, he and his group were now under surveillance by government authorities. Well, given both the timeframe and the climate, it should have been glaringly obvious: the authorities saw King's words (and those of his claimed Martian friends) as nothing less than outright propaganda designed to make the U.K. government look bad and the Russians look good. In a letter of May 26, King scolded Scotland Yard and did his utmost to try and put things straight. He wrote in his letter that the Aetherius Society was actually "a religious and occult society, which has contact with Intelligences on certain other planets. We are non-political and non-sectarian." That's certainly not how the authorities saw things, though.

As to how Special Branch became involved in all of this weirdness, and learned of the activities and statements of King, well, that's all very simple. *The Empire News* was very much a right-wing newspaper. King's political views were anything *but* right-wing. It transpires that one of the staff of *The Empire News*, concerned and pissed that King was using his *Cosmic Voice* publication to promote communism, contacted Scotland Yard just a couple of days before their planned article on King appeared. According to Special Branch, their source at the publication "wished to bring it to the notice of this department in view of the, in his opinion, Communist bias of part of the contents which refer to the atom bomb."

The result was that Scotland Yard opened a file on King and his colleagues. They did much more than that, though. After receiving King's letter of disgust as to how his organization was being portrayed and presented, on May 31 an officer headed out to King's home. The matter of King, his motivations, the goals of the Aetherius Society, the comments concerning Russia and nuclear weapons, and alien life were discussed frankly – and surreally, too. The Special Branch officer who had the task of speaking with King wrote the following summarized "Special Report:"

"I disclosed my identity and told King that I had come to see him in connection with his letter to the Commissioner. I pointed out to him that in this letter he stated 'The article purports to give a report of some recent work of this Society and states that the Society is being scrutinized by the Special Branch of Scotland Yard,' whereas the article states, 'The 'warning' – in a special issue of the magazine – is being scrutinized by Scotland Yard's Special Branch.'

Many might say – justifiably – that there is very little difference between scrutinizing the words of the "warning" and scrutinizing the work of the Aetherius Society. The head-to-head at King's home was just about as cordial as it could have been. From then on, however, and for a couple of years, King and his followers were watched intensely. Interestingly, Special Branch officers took careful studies of King's written output, too. Take note of the following, prepared by a Special Branch officer in May 1957:

COSMIC VOICE (Special Emergency May 1957) consists of a cover page and three pages of cyclostyle printed matter stapled together and is printed and published by THE AETHERIUS SOCIETY, 88, The Drive Mansions, Fulham Road, S.W.6. In page 1 of the printed matter one George KING is referred to as the Chairman of the society.

On page 1, which is headed "Introduction. You are responsible," it is stated that KING is able to tune in telepathically to mental radiations from a Space Station in the orbit of the Earth, 1550 miles above its surface, which is controlled by an entity from the Planet Mars, referred to as Mars Sector 6. It also states that an appeal for the cessation of nuclear experimentation was transmitted on the 7th May, 1957 from the Space Station. Pages 2 and 3 give the text of this message in full. In brief, it is an appeal to the ordinary man to protest through spiritual progress against nuclear bombs.

Reference is made on page 1 *to the placing of blame by the West on Russia* [italics mine] because it is said that it is necessary to make weapons for protection against this country, and the question is asked, "Yet, Western Civilizations, have not the latest Peace moves come from this country you condemn." The trend of the text is more religious than political in general. KING is obviously a crank.

King claimed that some 600 copies of the Special Emergency Supplement of "COSMIC VOICE" dated 7th May, 1957 has been printed, and that copies had been sent to Buckingham Palace, No. 10, Downing Street, President Eisenhower at Washington, to 125 Members of Parliament, Prime Ministers of the Dominions, etc., as well as to Religious and Social Reform authorities and to many newspapers.

Special Branch certainly viewed King as, in their words, a "crank." As the extract from the previously-classified document above shows, however, they also came to quickly realize that he was highly motivated when it came to getting the word out regarding his views on nuclear weapons and the Russians. That alone was certainly a matter of deep concern to the authorities. The surveillance continued at a steady and secret pace. Another Special Branch document, from 1959, provides the following on the Aetherius Society: "It crusades for the suspension of the H-bomb tests and supports the Campaign for Nuclear Disarmament. It took part in the 1958 Aldermaston March and holds public meetings from time to time. One was held on 23rd August 1959 when 200 persons formed a 'quiet, amused' audience. It was covered by Special Branch."

The reference to the "Aldermaston March" is a highly important one, as will now become apparent.

An arm of the U.K. Government's Ministry of Defense, the Atomic Weapons Establishment – known informally as "Aldermaston" - is situated on what was previously a military base: Royal Air Force Aldermaston, Berkshire, England. It takes its name from the village that is home to the AWE. It's important to note that in the late 1950s there was a great deal of concern on the part of the people of the U.K. that, in the event of a nuclear confrontation between the United States and the Soviet Union, the U.K. would also end up getting dragged into the maelstrom and, inevitably, totally wiped off the map, too. The outcome of these concerns was that more and more people chose to take a highly proactive approach to making their concerns and fears known to the government of the day. This was largely due to the creation, in 1957, of the Campaign for Nuclear Disarmament (CND). Its president was the renowned writer, political activist, and socialist, Bertrand Russell.

In an effort to highlight their views and worries relative to ever-growing nuclear proliferation, the CND decided to organize what became known as the "Aldermaston Marches." The public was encouraged to hit the road – on foot – and head off from London to the AWE facility in the sleepy little village of Aldermaston, which dates back to the 12th century and that, today, has a population of barely one thousand. The first such march took place on the Easter weekend of April 4-7, 1958. It was a significant event, one that let the U.K. Government know that not everyone was in accord with officialdom's policy on nukes.

Several thousand people took to the highways and the byways, all to have their say. Loudly. The presence and actions of the CND clearly had sizeable numbers of the people of the U.K. all revved up and ready to go. As evidence of this, in the march of 1960, more than sixty thousand people turned up at Trafalgar Square, London, with more than *one hundred thousand* making the trek to Aldermaston. Members of the Aetherius Society took a proactive part in *every* march from 1958 to 1965. Such was the CND's satisfaction with the first weekend of protest, the march became a yearly event: it continued until 1965 and was briefly resurrected in 1972. One of those who was a regular fixture at the marches was Michael Foot. He was a U.K. Member of Parliament who crusaded against nuclear weapons. Foot was also the leader of the Labor Party from 1980 to 1983 and gave his backing to the CND. We'll come back to Michael Foot imminently. You'll see why.

It was certainly the case that the Aldermaston marches largely went ahead with an absolute minimum of violence. U.K. authorities, though, were concerned by the possibility that the demonstrations just might have been secretly infiltrated by "Communist agitators;" even by Russian operatives, passing themselves off as members of the U.K. public and doing their utmost to whip up a frenzy and to get the lowdown on the CND. Both MI5 (the U.K.'s equivalent of the FBI) and MI6 (the U.K.'s CIA) were deeply worried that the Russians had wormed their way into the hearts of the CND and those who were coordinating the annual marches to Aldermaston. Those suspicions were amplified – and perhaps even vindicated - when, in the 1980s, damning data surfaced on the aforementioned Michael Foot.

Oleg Gordievsky was born in Moscow, Russia in 1938 and received training with The People's Commissariat for Internal Affairs (the NKVD). In 1963, he joined the KGB, achieving the rank of colonel. Gordievsky was soon posted to the Soviet Embassy in Copenhagen, Denmark. It was while he was stationed in the city that Gordievsky became very disillusioned by his time spent in the KGB; to the extent that he decided there was only one cause of action he could take: Gordievsky carefully planned on secretly working for the other side, the West. The Danish Security Intelligence Service took deep note of Gordievsky. They wasted no time in contacting their counterparts in MI6. Staff at MI6 were informed that Gordievsky just might be willing to switch sides, albeit with him still appearing to be faithful to his controllers in the KGB. MI6 was quick to react. Until the mid-1980s, Gordievsky played the role of dutiful KGB officer, but all the time he was leaking classified, and important, material to British intelligence. It didn't last, though. Everything came crashing down in 1985, which was when Gordievsky's cover was finally blown. He was soon back in Moscow, going through nothing but brutal interrogation. The future looked bleak; very bleak. It turned out, however, that matters were not so bad, after all. In July 1985 Gordievsky was smuggled out of Russia, into Finland, and then onto the U.K., via Norway. It would be more than half a decade before Gordievesky's family could follow him. All of which brings us back to the controversies surrounding Michael Foot.

Gordievsky reeled off an astounding amount of material that provoked wide-eyes and jaw-dropping gasps within MI6's corridors of power. One of the many revelations was that the KGB had a relationship with Michael Foot. Not only that, Foot had been secretly paid by the KGB to provide information on the Aldermaston marches and on the Campaign for Nuclear Disarmament, both to which Foot was deeply connected. Although the *Sunday Times* newspaper was sued by Foot – successfully, it must be stressed – for printing such claims, it's a fact that the rest of Gordievsky's extensive revelations proved to be true. Now, in conclusion, we return to the Aetherius Society and a few salient points:

- Special Branch recorded that George King's alien-driven organization "crusades for the suspension of the H-bomb."
- The members of the Aetherius Society took part in the Aldermaston marches that KGB asset Michael Foot also took part in.
- The Aetherius Society gave its support to the Campaign for Nuclear Disarmament.
- The marches, those on them, and the CND had been targeted by the KGB, as had Michael Foot, something that Oleg Gordievsky noted.
- One can easily see why Special Branch kept their beady eyes on George King and his followers. Taking into consideration the threads above, who in the intelligence community wouldn't have?

Now, let's forge ahead, but still on the matter of the Cold War. As a result of the seriously fraught situation that existed between the United States and Cuba in the early 1960s, U.S. intelligence did its utmost to try and find ways to oust Fidel Castro from power. One such early-1960s-era operation is almost hard to believe. While it didn't involve UFOs, it most certainly did revolve around the faking of a supernatural entity in the skies over Cuba; and so, in that sense, it's highly relevant to the overall story. It provides us with yet another example of how the world of the paranormal was utilized by intelligence agencies to do its utmost to manipulate world events. Before we get to the program itself, a bit of background data is required.

Staff at the John F. Kennedy Presidential Library say: "In 1959, Fidel Castro came to power in an armed revolt that overthrew Cuban dictator Fulgencio Batista. The U.S. government distrusted Castro and was wary of his relationship with Nikita Khrushchev, the leader of the Soviet Union. Before his inauguration, John F. Kennedy was briefed on a plan by the Central Intelligence Agency (CIA) developed during the Eisenhower administration to train Cuban exiles for an invasion of their homeland. The plan anticipated that the Cuban people and elements of the Cuban military would support the invasion. The ultimate goal was the overthrow of Castro and the establishment of a non-communist government friendly to the United States."

The CIA provides important data on the U.S.-Cuba situation in this same time-frame:

"The establishment of a Communist state 90 miles off the coast of Florida raised obvious security concerns in Washington and did not sit well with President Eisenhower. In February 1960, Cuba signed an agreement to buy oil from the Soviet Union. When the U.S.-owned refineries in the country refused to process the oil, Castro seized the firms, and the U.S. broke off diplomatic relations with the Cuban regime. To the chagrin of the Eisenhower administration, Castro established increasingly close ties with the Soviet Union while delivering fiery condemnations of the U.S. The American-Cuban relationship deteriorated further when Castro established diplomatic relations with our Cold War rival, the Soviet Union. Castro and Soviet Premier Nikita Khrushchev signed a series of pacts that resulted in large deliveries of economic and military aid in 1960. Within a year, Castro proclaimed himself a communist, formally allied his country with the Soviet

Union, and seized remaining American and foreign-owned assets. Eisenhower authorized the CIA to conduct a covert operation to rid the island of its self-appointed leader. The CIA formulated a plan to recruit Cuban exiles living in the Miami area. It would train and equip the exiles to infiltrate Cuba and start a revolution to ignite an uprising across the island and overthrow Castro."

It didn't work out quite like that, as the ill-fated, disastrous outcome of the Bay of Pigs invasion of April 1961 - designed to get rid of Castro - demonstrated. Things got worse in October 1962. That was when the Cuban Missile Crisis almost plunged the world into a civilization-ending nuclear war. It was in this period that a military figure, renowned for his ability to think out of the box to an incredible degree, got involved in the attempts to have Castro removed from power. That man was Major General Edward Geary Lansdale. His career was long, notable and extremely alternative. In the Second World War, Lansdale spent a great deal of time working for the Office of Strategic Services. The OSS – with its spies and "secret-agents" – was the inspiration for the CIA, which was created two years after the end of the war.

When Hitler and his hordes were finally defeated, Lansdale headed off to the Philippines, specifically to Headquarters Air Forces Western Pacific. Eight years later, he took a position in the Office of the Secretary of Defense. Lansdale became the Deputy Assistant to the SoD. It was while he was in the office that Lansdale really demonstrated his flair for all things off the wall. Perhaps the weirdest of all of Lansdale's strange ideas was a plan to fake a "Second Coming" of Jesus Christ in the skies over Cuba! The story can be found in a November 20, 1975 document with the lengthy title of *Alleged Assassination Plots Involving Foreign Leaders: Interim Report of the Select Committee to Study Government*

Operations with Respect to Intelligence Activities. It contains the curious testimony of a man named Thomas A. Parrott, who died at the age of ninety-two in 2007.

Parrott was, as the staff who run the website of the Arlington Cemetery, note: "...a former official with the Central Intelligence Agency and a member of several hospital boards and citizen group. Mr. Parrott spent 24 years with the CIA and was Assistant Deputy Director for National Intelligence Programs. Early in his career, he was Deputy Chief of the Soviet Division of the Clandestine Services Unit, a base chief in Germany and an assistant to CIA Director Allen Dulles."

As far as Lansdale's mind-blowing idea is concerned, Parrott had this to say to the Select Committee in 1975: "I'll give you one example of Lansdale's perspicacity. He had a wonderful plan for getting rid of Castro. This plan consisted of spreading the word that the Second Coming of Christ was imminent and that Christ was against Castro who was anti-Christ. And you would spread this word around Cuba, and then on whatever date it was, that there would be a manifestation of this thing. At the time – this was absolutely true – and at the time just over the horizon, there would be an American submarine that would surface off of Cuba and send up some star-shells. This would be the manifestation of the Second Coming and Castro would be overthrown."

For those who may not know, star-shells are powerful flares used by military agencies, chiefly to light up the night-skies. Lansdale didn't just bring star-shells to the table, however. His plan was to recruit a crack-team of U.S. Navy personnel who would be integral players in the operation. They would approach the coastal areas in fleets of small submarines, which would then project huge pictures of Jesus onto the clouds over Cuba, and as close as possible to the capital city of Havana. Lansdale was still not finished. He also planned to have compact aircraft fly with their engines muffled and hidden by those same clouds – and then broadcast the "voice of Jesus" via a number of powerful loud-speakers. The message was going to be clear and to-the-point: renounce Castro and embrace the West. The operation, however, proved to be too difficult to successfully execute and it was ultimately shelved. The plan, though, does show one important thing when it came to national security-based issues: that during the Cold War, UFOs were not the only high-flying, supernatural phenomena that intelligence agencies deemed ripe for manipulation.

12.

"THERE IS SOME COMMUNIST INFLUENCE IN THE BUREAU"

It was not just the intelligence services of the United States and the United Kingdom who were concerned by the activities of certain controversial figures in Ufology with provable ties to communism. The Australian government did very much likewise. The situation was spreading and spiraling. Like a bad rash, too. A *red* rash, of course. Previously-classified documentation placed into the public domain by the Commonwealth of Australia demonstrates that more than a few characters in the flying saucer scene of the fifties, sixties and seventies had links to the menacing commies. But, were those links purely innocent in nature? Or, incredibly, were Australia's UFO sleuths – or, at least, *some* of them – in league with sinister figures operating right out of the very heart of the Kremlin itself? For national security reasons, the answers to those questions were sorely needed. And they *were* found.

Australia's Freedom of Information Act has revealed that the vast majority of all the spying on the nation's alien-seekers in the early days of the Cold War was undertaken by the ASIO: the Australian Security Intelligence Organization. Imagine the CIA meets the National Security Agency meets the U.K.'s Special Branch, and you'll have a good idea of the structure and work of the ASIO. Not to mention the overwhelming secrecy surrounding it. The ASIO state of their long-running organization that its creation was directly driven by the unsettling fact that, as far back as the late 1940s, Soviet agents were already prowling around Australia: infiltrating, machinating, and doing all they could to cause problems for the people of Australia and its government.

The ASIO's staff state the following of the agency's creation and early history:

When Prime Minister Ben Chifley established ASIO by charter in 1949, Australia and other Western nations had emerged from the Second World War and were grappling with a different kind of threat - Soviet interference.

These were the early days of the Cold War. A series of decoded Soviet cables—known as the Venona intercepts—confirmed Soviet spies were active in Australia, prompting the United States (US) and the United Kingdom (UK) to suspend the sharing of intelligence with us. Great Britain sought Australia's commitment to establish a more rigorous internal security intelligence regime.

David Horner, author of *The Spy Catchers: the Official History of ASIO 1949–1963* explains: "American and British cryptanalysts deciphered the encrypted cabled messages between the headquarters of the Soviet intelligence service, the KGB, and its resident intelligence officers in embassies around the world. This Venona intelligence, as it was known, revealed the existence of a Soviet spy ring in Australia, and ASIO was then set up to try to catch the spies. The Venona program was extremely secret and over the succeeding years ASIO spent much effort in trying to protect knowledge of its existence."

The Australian Government was urged to establish a security service modelled on the UK's MI5, and so Australian military intelligence chiefs and the senior politicians of the day worked to establish ASIO. Prime Minister Ben Chifley appointed Justice Geoffrey Reed, a Supreme Court judge from South Australia, to establish the service, and in early 1949 oversaw the drafting of a charter to specify the role and functions of the Organization. ASIO's Charter empowered this new organization to undertake intelligence activities for the protection of the Commonwealth against espionage, sabotage and subversion. The first ASIO officers—only 15 in July 1949—set about investigating a number of people suspected of spying for the Soviets.

In light of all the above from the ASIO, it's hardly surprising that, from the 1950s onward, its personnel took a very close look at what UFO enthusiasts were saying and doing in Australia. And, most important of all, *why*. The outcome was that a handful of Australians were flagged as what, today, we would call "people of interest." It scarcely needs noting that no-one should aspire to become one of them. As in *ever*. We'll begin with the strange saga of a man named Stan Seers. UFO authority Timothy Good states: "In 1959 Stan Steers, President of the Queensland Flying Saucer Research Bureau [which was created in 1956] at the time received a phone call from a man requesting a meeting in a large car park in Brisbane, hinting that Seers might learn something to his advantage about UFOs."

Seers, by his own admission, at first thought that this was someone's idea of a not too amusing practical joke. All thoughts of pranks went quickly out of the window, however, when – after a couple more phone calls with the mysterious man at the other end of the line – Seers was finally able to meet the clandestine character at that aforementioned car park. He was nothing less than an employee of the ASIO. "Mr. D," as Seers tantalizingly termed

the man, was seemingly intent on playing a game of "bad-cop"-
"good-cop," but all on his lonesome. The ASIO agent began in
somewhat hostile fashion and "dangled the Communist bogey,"
as Seers succinctly put it. The man then proceeded to reel off
significant background information on both Seers and two of his
colleagues in the QFSRB. In an instant, Seers realized something
amazing and more than a bit alarming: *I'm being watched. Closely.
By the Government. Shit.*

Mr. D's tone soon changed, though, when he suggested to Seers
that perhaps the ASIO could provide significant UFO-themed
data to Seers and his friends – if and when the circumstances
were deemed to be right; whatever that meant. The Australian
government handing its UFO files over to a group of ufologists?
It sounded way too good to be true. No surprise: it turns out
that's *exactly* what it was. Mr. D carefully, skillfully and ultimately
ruthlessly wormed his way into the UFO group, causing major
dissention in the ranks, and fracturing friendships as he did so.
This is what Seers astutely came to believe was the entire point
of the operation: to infiltrate the QFSRB, to weaken it, and to
ensure that the ASIO was able to keep a careful watch on it and
its members at all times – and particularly so those in the group
who had what was referred to as by the ASIO as having "some
Communist influence." A declassified ASIO document, titled *The
Queensland Flying Saucer Research Bureau*, and dated August 4, 1959
– the very same time-frame in which Stan Seers was approached
– reveals that the ASIO had undertaken a wealth of background
data on the UFO group, as the following extract shows:

> The Queensland Flying Saucer Research Bureau is an
> organization with a present membership of 163 that meets
> regularly on the second Wednesday of each month in the
> Canberra Hotel and conducts a discussion group on the

first Wednesday of each month in…Elizabeth Street, Brisbane. The members are of great diversity in outlook, politics and religion but all have a common purpose in endeavoring to establish the authenticity of unidentified flying objects which have been sighted throughout the world, including Australia, particularly in the last ten years.

There is some Communist influence in the Bureau due to the presence of the Secretary, Gordon Leslie Jamieson, and members of the Souwer family of Slacks Creek, to whom he is related by marriage.

Recently an announcement appeared in the daily papers that stated a difference of opinion had arisen amongst two groups of eminent Soviet physicists concerning the origin of an explosion which took place in Siberia in 1908 [the controversial "Tunguska" affair.] For the past fifty years, it was accepted as the landing of a giant meteorite. A difference has arisen due to the fact that a small group of scientists have now put forward the theory that due to the unnatural nature of the explosion and the fact that a large number of persons in the area suffered from leukemia, the explosion could have been the destruction of some space vehicle, possibly trying to land or in some mechanical trouble.

At the May meeting of the Bureau, Gordon Leslie Jamison had prepared for dispatch to the Soviet Union a letter asking for any additional information that may be available from the scientists. To date, no reply has been received but it is quite possible that with the re-introduction of the Soviet Embassy to Australia this could easily afford an avenue for contact between the V.O.K.S. representative and the Bureau with offers from the Soviet Embassy to assist in the supply of information.

The ASIO's concerns about VOKS - Vsesojuznoe obschestvo kul'turnykh svyzei s zagranitsei - liaising with the QFSRB were completely valid and warranted. DocumentsTalk.com states that VOKS was, and I quote, "a Soviet organization that promoted cultural contacts with foreign countries from 1925 to 1958. Established in 1925 as an important Soviet propaganda vehicle abroad, VOKS was formally a public association involving the participation of Soviet scientists, writers, artists, musicians, actors, educators and sportsmen...By 1957, societies for friendship with the USSR had been established in 47 nations."

All well and good. Or, so it seems. There is, however, the following from DocumentsTalk.com, which should be noted carefully: "...VOKS also often served as a convenient 'roof' for operations of both branches of Soviet intelligence, whose residents and operatives used opportunities provided by VOKS to establish and maintain contacts in intellectual, scientific and government circles. *These contacts were, for the most part, unaware that they were dealing not with 'cultural representatives' and diplomats, but with intelligence officers* [italics mine]."

The ASIO was fully aware that VOKS was filled to the absolute brim with agents of the Soviet Union, and not just with cultural representatives. And, although the VOKS program was shut down in 1958, the QFSRB had been in existence since 1956. Two years was an ample amount of time for the UFO group to have cultivated a chain of communication with VOKS, something that the ASIO feared just might already have happened. It's not surprising then that the ASIO became very concerned that those same Soviet agents could have tried to "turn" one or more QFSRB members. And, in a worst-case scenario, *did* turn them. Such a grim picture was seen as being disturbingly all too possible. For example, although Stan Steers was described by the ASIO as being "the most level headed and rational member of the Bureau," the QFSRB's secretary, Gordon Jamieson, and his family were referred to bluntly and concisely as "pacifists and communists."

Also of some concern to the ASIO was one Ricky Royal. He was a pilot during the Second World War. UFO Research Queensland note the following: "In 1944, while flying over Bass Strait in a Beaufort Bomber, Ricky saw a dark shadow, belching flame from its rear which then flew parallel to his plane while remaining at a distance of 100-150ft. This object paced him for approximately 18 minutes then accelerated to 3 times the speed of Ricky's plane, emitting 100 feet to 150 feet of flames while doing so. Ricky estimated its speed to be 235mph flying at an elevation of 4500ft. Soon after he submitted a report to The Australian Flying Saucer Research Society describing what must have been a terrifying experience for a 29 year old during wartime. This incident inspired Ricky to spend the next 25 years of his life involved in UFO research during which time he, along with other interested members of the public, established the Queensland Flying Saucer Research Bureau in Redcliffe, Queensland in 1956."

Regarding Royal, the ASIO was fully aware of the fact that as late as 1959 he retained significant numbers of contacts in the Australian military. The ASIO's personnel, whether justified or not, came up with a fascinating theory: that Soviet intelligence agents just might consider hanging in front of Royal's wide eyes a bunch of amazing - but completely fabricated - tales and documents of UFOs seen in Russia. And what might those Soviet operatives want in return? Australian military secrets, that's what; secrets that Royal just might be willing to try and secure from friends and former colleagues still in the Air Force. And all so that Royal could get his hands on a bunch of material on UFOs in the Soviet Union; material that had been ingeniously crafted by disinformation specialists in Moscow. It's *very* important to stress that while the ASIO did not find *any* wrongdoing on Royal's part, they noted in the 1959 files that Royal was, when it came to UFOs, someone who "*would resort to any means to obtain information concerning them* [italics mine]." From the perspective of the ASIO, that did not bode well in the slightest. This nightmarish scenario of "faked-UFO-tales-in-return-for-real-military-secrets" would resurface on the other side of the world – the United States, specifically - in the late 1970s, as we'll see later.

And then there was Sonja Lyubicin.

One of the more intriguing, but lesser known, of the 1950s-era Contactees, Sonja Lyubicin was a woman who had a background and a life filled with mystery, adventure and intrigue. In 1956, she claimed to have been taken on a trip to Saturn by the Space Brothers. To her eternal delight, Lyubicin found that the people of the huge, ringed planet were highly "sexually active" and particularly liked hosting swinging parties, which is a far cry from the grim encounters that people report with today's small, black-eyed "Grey" aliens! She also had a connection to George Adamski. The whispered word on the galactic grapevine was that during a wild orgy in Australia, Lyubicin got nailed by none other than Orthon himself! UFO historians Adam Gorightly and Greg Bishop say of this entertaining saga that the party "...was arranged by free swinging Orthon and involved 32 other spacemen for whom... the women performed 'their sexual bidding.'" Beats the grim scene at the site of the Roswell crash, right?

A close encounter or several of the sexual kind? To be sure! If we are to take Lyubicin's at her word, that is. Lyubicin also claimed deep contacts within the very heart of the U.S. government, even maintaining that she had spent time attending top secret meetings on UFOs at the White Sands Missile Range, New Mexico. How much of Lyubicin's story was true is anyone's guess. It's notable, though, that the ASIO decided to open a file on her. In part, that dossier provides these words:

> A member of the [Queensland Flying Saucer Research] Bureau who was extremely active during the visit of George Adamski was a Sonja Ljubicin [sic], a naturalized Australian of Yugoslav origin, who previously resided at...Ann Street, Valley. This person was carried away to the extent that she believed she had travelled in a space-craft to other planets. On the 16th July 1959 she left her employment and travelling on an Australian passport No. K235116 issued on the 29th June 1959 at Brisbane travelled by Qantas Flight EM. 742 from Sydney on the 21st July 1959 to the United States of America to join George Adamski.

UFO investigator Hakan Blomqvist, said of Lyubicin that she, "...continued living in California and on July 12, 1979 married William Paul Appleton. She then changed her name to Sonya Appleton. They eventually settled in Honolulu, Hawaii where the marriage ended. Sonya died in Honolulu, just before her 63rd birthday, July 2, 1989."

It should be noted that the primary reason why the ASIO had Lyubicin in their sights – and kept abreast of her activities – was because of her background. Namely, that she was born and, until the age of twenty, lived in Yugoslavia; a country that in 1946 became the communist Federal People's Republic of Yugoslavia. While Lyubicin and her family fled Yugoslavia in 1947, there were some agents of the ASIO who pondered on the possibility that she might have had Communist leanings. Whether or not this was a case of the ASIO reaching just a bit too far, we'll likely never know. But, that the QFSRB was an organization which had a number of Communists in its ranks – and who may very well have had communications with Soviet agents via the VOKS system – meant it was all but inevitable that Lyubicin would become the subject of deep surveillance. How deep, exactly? Well, put it like this: we can see from the now-available material on Lyubicin that the ASIO knew all about her plans to fly to the United States; they had the names of the relevant airlines. They even knew the flight-numbers and had her Australian passport number on file. Whatever the truth behind Sonja Lyubicin's controversial claims, they were certainly enough to make the ASIO sit up and take notice. And that's exactly what its agents did.

The final word on the QFSRB – also from August 1959 - goes to the ASIO: "At present the Queensland Bureau does not appear to constitute any serious concern, mainly due to the control exercised by the President, Seers, *but its activities will be constantly watched* as there is the ever present possibility that with the loss of Seers' guidance as President, *together with Soviet contact and any increased Communist Party of Australia membership, the Bureau could become of far greater interest* [italics mine]."

It's worth noting that George Adamski was also watched closely by intelligence agencies in 1959 – and, in part, in relation to the matter of Russia and communism and a certain trip he made overseas. In early 1959, Adamski was invited to deliver a series of lectures in New Zealand: specifically in Wellington and Auckland. Notably, this lecture-tour was of interest to the world of government, and his presentations were clandestinely scrutinized by government operatives. A Foreign Service Dispatch of February 1959 was sent from the American Embassy in New Zealand to the Department of State in Washington, D.C., that summarized

Adamski's activities in New Zealand. Also forwarded to the FBI, the CIA, the Air Force and the Navy, the report was titled "'Flying Saucer' Expert Lecturing In New Zealand" and recorded the following, amusing information:

Mr. George Adamski, the Californian "flying saucer expert" and author of the book *Flying Saucers Have Landed* and others, has been visiting New Zealand for the last two weeks. He has given well-attended public lectures in Auckland and Wellington as well as meetings with smaller groups of "saucer" enthusiasts. In Wellington his lecture filled the 2,200 seats in the Town Hall. He was not permitted to charge for admission as the meeting was held on a Sunday night, but a "silver coin" collection was taken up and this would more than recoup his expenses.

Adamski's lectures appear to cover the usual mass of sighting reports, pseudo-scientific arguments in support of his theories and his previously well-publicized "contacts" with saucers and men from Venus. He is repeating his contention that men from other planets are living anonymously on the earth and, according to the press, said in Auckland that there may be as many as 40,000,000 of these in total. He is also making references to security restrictions and saying that the U.S. authorities know a lot more than they will tell. The report of Adamski's lecture in Wellington in The Dominion was flanked by an article by Dr. I.L. THOMPSON, Director of the Carter Observatory, vigorously refuting Adamski on a number of scientific points. However, the news report of the lecture called it "the best Sunday night's entertainment Wellington has seen for quite a time."

Quite! Moving on, there is this from the authorities who had Adamski under surveillance:

> Interest in flying saucers in New Zealand seems to be roughly comparable to that in the United States. There is a small but active organization which enthusiasts have supported for some years. This organization publishes a small paper and receives and circulates stories of sightings. At the Adamski lecture in Wellington, approximately 40 members of the 'Adamski Corresponding Society' wore blue ribbons and sat in reserved seats in the front row. Press reports suggest that Adamski probably is making no new converts to saucer credence in his current tour. His audiences have given forth with a certain amount of 'incredulous murmuring' and are said to be totally unimpressed with his pictures of saucers.

In late 1959, Adamski was yet again the topic of FBI interest when an unidentified American citizen offered an opinion that Adamski was using the UFO controversy as a means to promote communism. In a report on the affair, the FBI recorded the following:

> [Censored] said that in recent weeks she and her husband had begun to wonder if Adamski is subtly spreading Russian propaganda. She said that, according to Adamski, the "space people" are much better people than those on earth; that they have told him the earth is in extreme danger from nuclear tests and that they must be stopped; that they have found peace under a system in which churches, schools, individual governments, money, and private property were abolished in favor of a central

governing council, and nationalism and patriotism have been done away with; that the 'space people' want nuclear tests stopped immediately and that never should people on earth fight; if attacked, they should lay down their arms and welcome their attackers.

[Censored] said the particular thing that first made her and her husband wonder about Adamski was a letter they received from him dated 10/12/59, in which it was hinted that the Russians receive help in their outer space programs from the "space people," and that the "space people" will not help any nation unless such nation has peaceful intent. It occurred to them that the desires and recommendations of the "space people" whom Adamski quotes are quite similar to Russia's approach, particularly as to the ending of nuclear testing, and it was for this reason she decided to call the FBI.

Moving onto the 1960s and away from Adamski and New Zealand, and back to Australia, there is an enlightening file contained in the ASIC archives that has the lengthy title of *Australian Flying Saucer Research Society, Allegations of attempted take-over by pro-Communist Sydney group.* Prepared by one K. Cotton of the Special Branch division of Police Headquarters, Adelaide, South Australia, and dated January 4, 1962, it begins as follows:

I have to report that recently Fred Stone, former President of the Australian Flying Saucer Research Society, called at this Branch and stated that his organization feared that they were in danger of being taken over by a Sydney group known as the Unidentified Flying Object Investigation Centre, whose headquarters were situated in Sydney, New South Wales.

Former members of the Adelaide committee, who resigned on the 3rd November 1961, were concerned at this maneuver as they believed the Sydney society was "pink" in outlook and atheistic in attitude, a fact which Stone had confirmed to his own satisfaction on previous visits to that State.

Before we continue with the content of the document, it's worth knowing, for those who may be unaware, what, precisely, the term "pink" meant back then. RationalWiki notes: "'Pinko commie' is a phrase used in parodies or mockeries of opponents of communism, particularly those from the McCarthy era. 'Pinko' refers to someone who is not himself or herself a communist but who sympathizes with communism (hence 'pink,' not quite red). Consequently 'pinko commie' is arguably (logically) an oxymoron. The phrase started gaining popularity as a description of the communist movement as early as the 1930s."

With that said, back to the document:

Stone stated that the present unrest had been instigated by Mrs. J. Ingram-Moore, otherwise known as June Marsden, a member of the UFO Society, who resides in New South Wales, but who has recently visited Adelaide lecturing on Flying Saucers. During the conversation Mr. Stone mentioned the following persons, whom he said were, or had been, connected with such matters in New South Wales:- Andrew Tomas, Editor of the *UFO* magazine, an accountant employed by Hookers of Sydney, Dr. Lindtner, a veterinary surgeon, and an ex-Polish pilot, who was employed by the C.S.I.R.O in Sydney, a former Vice-President of the UFO. Mr. Clifford, a retired Dental Surgeon of Sydney.

As neither the UFO society, nor the persons mentioned as connected with it, had previously come under the notice of this Branch, a request was made to Sydney Special Branch as to whether the society or the people had come under their notice.

Files were opened on Lindtner, Clifford and Tomas; the latter was born in St. Petersburg, Russia. He was someone who had a deep interest in the matter of what today has become popularly known as "ancient aliens." His books included *Atlantis: From Legend to Discovery*; *On the Shores of Endless Worlds*; *We Are Not the First*; and *Shambhala: Oasis of Light*. As for the aforementioned Dr. Lindtner, we have the following from the ASIO's Special Branch:

> The Unidentified Flying Object Investigation Center has not previously come under the notice of this Branch. The only person referred to in the attached report who has previously come under notice at this Branch is Dr. Lindtner, born at Ljubljana, Yugoslavia, on the 30.8.1920, arrived in Australia, who is identified hereunder...He first came under notice in 1954 when it was reported that about two years prior to then he had been seen at the Russian Social Club, Sydney. In 1955 he was reported to be a member of the Committee of the Russian Social Club. In 1961 he came under notice as President of the "Yugal" Soccer Club, which is alleged by anti-Communist Yugoslavian immigrants to be sponsored by the Yugoslav CVonsul at Sydney and to be composed of pro-Tito Yuogslavs.

The Encyclopedia of World Biography says of Yugoslav statesman Marshal Tito: "The Yugoslav statesman Marshal Tito became president of Yugoslavia in 1953. He directed the rebuilding of a

Yugoslavia devastated in World War II and the bringing together of Yugoslavia's different peoples until his death in 1980."

And *Your Dictionary* states: "From 1945 to 1953 Tito acted as prime minister and minister of defense in the government, whose most dramatic political action was the capture, trial, and execution of Gen. Mihajlović in 1946. Between 1945 and 1948 Tito led his country through an extreme and ruthless form of dictatorship in order to mold Yugoslavia into a socialist state modeled after the Soviet Union. In January 1953, he was named first president of Yugoslavia and president of the Federal Executive Council; the 1963 Constitution named him president for life."

Yet again, we see why, exactly, Australian security personnel were so keen to put all of the pieces together when it came to the strange UFO jigsaw in their midst: seemingly, there were Russian and communist links just about everywhere. It's intriguing to note Officer Cotton's final words on this issue of communist infiltration of an Australia-based UFO research group: "In view of the above information, it would appear that *Mr. Stone's fears may not be entirely groundless* [italics mine], and future intelligence obtained regarding the composition of the Australian Flying Saucer Research Society will be transmitted to A.S.I.C. Perhaps this report might now be forwarded to the Regional Director, 'D' Branch, Adelaide, for his information."

Although, I do think that having concerns about a local soccer team is taking concerns just a bit too far!

Moving onto the decade of the 1970s, the fear – whether valid or sculpted by paranoia – that Australia's alien hunters were working hand-in-glove with the Russians led yet further secret surveillance to be undertaken. An ASIO document of October 11, 1972, provides us with this: "Colin Norris, the Public Relations Officer for the Australian Flying Saucer Research Society, who lives in

Adelaide, claims to be in correspondence with Soviet Academicians on the subject of unidentified flying objects (U.F.O.'s). Norris is [deleted] and works for the G.P.O. [General Post Office]."

Norris stated that he had, and I quote from the ASIO papers in the public domain, "no political interests." Maybe so, but ASIO agents recorded this: "Norris spoke to members of the Young Socialist League in South Australia about U.F.O.'s on the 14th November, 1969." Interestingly, two documents that are focused on the 1969 meeting are still withheld – and for reasons relative to national security. Many of the ASIO's general files on Australia's Young Socialist League remain unavailable, too. Connected or not, back in the late 1980s, and when I lived in England, I subscribed to Norris's UFO-themed magazine. When my airmailed copies arrived from Australia, they were always opened and resealed. No attempt was ever made to mask the fact that someone had taken a look at the contents. A message of sorts? Maybe.

13.

"BRITIƧH-RUƧƧIAN COOPERATION IN OBƧERVATION OF UFOƧ"

It's intriguing that in the mid-to-late part of the 1960s there occurred a great deal of activity in relation to Russian meddling and manipulation of the UFO arena. We'll begin with something that became known infamously as UMMO. It was during the 1960s that a man named Fernando Sesma, a Spanish UFO enthusiast, started to receive a wealth of strange "technical papers" through the mail. They were said to have been penned by the OEMII, the people of a faraway world known as UMMO. It wasn't long before close to a dozen additional people in Spain's UFO research community began to receive such material too. Sesma was a controversial contactee, someone who, in 1967, wrote a publication titled *UMMO, Otro Planeta Habitado* (*UMMO, Another Inhabited Planet*). Few, at first, took much notice of the strange affair of UMMO. But that soon changed.

Was Sesma really in touch with aliens? Let's see. Investigative writer Scott Corrales said: "In the mid 1950's, Jose Luis Jordan Pena [a Spanish communications technician who died in 2014 at the age of eighty-three] was elaborating the theory that paranoia was much more widespread among the population than psychiatrists of the time were willing to admit. Jordan Pena believed that no less than 79% of the population was afflicted, and proceeded to demonstrate the validity of his theory by concocting the UMMO affair - the story of tall, blond and friendly aliens who had landed near the French locality of Digne…

> "The perpetrator of the hoax of the century [Pena] penned his own confession in an article entitled 'UMMO: Otro Mito Que Hace Crash' for *La Alternativa Racional*, an Iberian equivalent of *The Skeptical Enquirer*. A believer in the concept of 'systematical paranoia,' Jordan Pena put forth beliefs that, in his own words, were imbued with a certain logic. He didn't limit himself to the theoretical framework, but actually took steps (by his own admission) to create a false landing in the Madrid suburb of Aluche, leaving bogus landing marks behind…"

Pena bolstered his hoaxed saga by claiming to have had his very own sighting of a flying saucer in the skies above the Spanish city of Madrid. Most notable of all, the UFO had a large emblem on the base of the craft. It was a cross with a half-circle on each side. Reportedly, a near-identical aerial vehicle of unidentified proportions was seen in May 1967, also in Madrid. This time, the saucer was caught on film. There is, however, very little doubt at all that the story – as well as the attendant photo – was bogus. It was not so much a deliberate, malicious hoax, though. Rather, it was more along the lines of a carefully-crafted program designed to demonstrate how belief-systems can be created, molded, and used to manipulate people – even on an extraordinarily large scale. On this latter point, the UMMO affair most assuredly did attract a huge following.

One of those who took a particular interest in the notoriety surrounding UMMO was the late Jim Keith, a conspiracy-theorist whose books included *Saucers of the Illuminati* and *Black Helicopters over America*. Keith also wrote *Casebook on the Men in Black*. In the pages of the latter book, Keith said: "The UMMO case was created through a large number of contacts – UFO sightings, personal contacts, messages through the mail and telephone – alleged to be from space brothers from the planet UMMO," which, Keith said, was "...located 14.6 light years from our solar system."

Keith also noted that the UMMO data was made up of "...six-to-ten page letters containing diagrams and equations, delineating UMMO science and philosophy. Differing from most channeled and beamed by space beings, they were scientifically savvy, although according to Jacques Vallee, smacked more of Euro sci-fi than superior extraterrestrial knowledge."

Keith too came to the conclusion that the whole UMMO affair was one huge grand hoax. He cited the words of a Spanish journalist named Manuel Carballal. It was Carballal, Keith said, who wrote that researchers Cales Berche, Jose J. Montejo and Javier Sierra had identified a well-known Spanish parapsychologist – who turned out to be none other than the aforementioned Jose Pena – as being the originator of the UMMO material. Keith expanded on this and stated that Pena "...is later reported to have admitted his creation of the complex hoax, stating that it had been a 'scientific experiment' aimed at testing the gullibility factor amongst Spanish UFO researchers."

As all of the above shows, there's very little doubt that UMMO was a fabrication – from the start to the finish. But, it wasn't quite the end, after all. There were those in the UFO research arena who suspected that the original UMMO hoax was, later on, ingeniously hijacked and expanded upon by certain official intelligence services - and, chiefly, the former Soviet Union's KGB. The scenario involved Russian operatives exploiting the original hoax as a cover for the dissemination of psychological warfare within the public UFO research community, as well as a means to secretly infiltrate and manipulate that same community to gather information.

Jacques Vallee stated of UMMO that, "…some of the data that was supposedly channeled from the UMMO organization in the sky was very advanced cosmology." He added that a portion of it "came straight out of the notes" of Andrei Sakharov, including what were described as "unpublished notes." Vallee also said that, "somebody had to have access to those notes, to inspire those messages, perhaps the KGB."

Andrei Sakharov – who died in 1989 – was a scientist who played an instrumental role in the development of the Soviet Union's hydrogen bomb program. He ultimately became, in the words of the Nobel Peace Committee, a spokesperson for the conscience of mankind. In 1975 Sakharov was awarded the prestigious Nobel Peace Prize. That the KGB might have decided to use the UMMO affair to its own, secret advantage, and to try and infiltrate and manipulate Ufology, sits nicely with what we have seen already with regard to the CIA's Robertson Panel and the attempts of the Soviets to secretly recruit Contactees like Orfeo Angelucci. But, when it came to UMMO, what was the exact goal of the Russians?

Jonathan Vankin and John Whalen, who penned the book *The 80 Greatest Conspiracies of All Time*, pondered on that very matter. They suggested the following: "Per Vallee, there are at least a couple of reasons: Cults are an ideal way to incubate ideas – and irrational belief systems – that might later prove destabilizing to enemy governments. Moreover, a cult might provide cover for foreign spies doing technical assessment; after all, the UMMO 'channelings' were distributed to noted Western scientists, who were encouraged to correspond with UMMOs representatives on Earth."

There's another, equally weird, story that *might* be connected to all of this. Jacques Vallee says: "The name UMMO may be hiding an inside joke. In 1970 a company called UMO Plant Hire, Ltd, was incorporated in Great Britain. It turned out to be a Soviet spy front. In September 1971, 105 Soviet officials were expelled from Britain for espionage, and UMO was closed down."

This is indeed a fact. On September 25, 1971, the U.K.'s *Guardian* newspaper ran an article that, in part, stated: "Britain is to expel 90 Soviet diplomats who have been engaged in active espionage, the Foreign Office announced last night. Another 15 Soviet officials, at present overseas, will not be allowed to return to this country. Many of these men are suspected of involvement in planning acts of sabotage. The expulsion order – affecting nearly 20 per cent of the 550 Soviet diplomats in Britain – is unprecedented in size and scope. It follows months of intensive investigation by the intelligence services, and the defection of a top KGB officer from the Soviet Embassy in London.

"The KGB man, who had the rank of major, proved the catalyst for the 'clearing' operation against Soviet espionage. He gave the security services a comprehensive breakdown of his country's espionage apparatus in Britain – and also supplied details '…of plans for infiltration of agents for the purposes of sabotage'", the Foreign Office said. In the opinion of Mr. Heath [the then-Prime-Minister] and Sir Alec Douglas-Home [who worked in the Foreign and Commonwealth Office] this crisis over diplomatic espionage by Soviet officials is so serious that the British Government cannot, and will not, enter into preparations for the European Security Conference proposed by the Soviet Union until the crisis is resolved."

The crisis was ultimately brought to an end, but for a long time, relations between the Soviet Union and the British Government were decidedly frosty.

As incredible as it may sound, in 1967 – which, bear in mind, was still the height of the Cold War – British authorities made a secret approach to the former Soviet Union's military. It was an approach that revolved around nothing less than UFOs. In fact, the British Government came straight to the point: they wished to clandestinely discuss the possibility of establishing a joint UK-Soviet UFO study-program. Sounds near-unbelievable? Yes, it does. But, it's one hundred percent verifiable. Thanks to the provisions of the U.S. Freedom of Information Act (FOIA), documentation has surfaced from the Defense Intelligence Agency that reveals at least significant parts of the story. According to the DIA: "In early 1967 (exact date believed to be 10 Nov) Moscow TV presented a program on Unidentified Flying Objects. On 12 Nov 67 a *Reuters* release in the U.K. (believe article was in *Daily Telegraph*) reported the TV program."

The essence of both the Soviet television show and the *Reuters* story, noted the DIA, was that "…the Russians had recently set up a commission to study UFOs." The chairman of the commission, the DIA learned, was a retired Soviet Air Force (SAF) Major General A.F. Stolyarov, a former Technical Services Officer. Not only that, the project had at its disposal no less than 18 astronomers and SAF officers and "200 observers."

A couple of days after the television production aired, the DIA learned, the *Reuters* correspondent paid Major General Stolyarov a visit. The general, recorded DIA personnel, "was very polite, confirmed the information about the commission, the 18 astronomers and SAF officers and the 200 observers. In addition, he said five positive sightings had been made."

One week later, however, things had changed significantly, as the DIA's files make very clear: "…the *Reuters* correspondent went back to see General Stolyarov. However, this time the correspondent could not get past the General's secretary, [and] was politely but firmly told the General was no longer available for interview."

But, then, there was a dramatic development in the story – and, probably, a wholly *unforeseen* development. The DIA uncovered information to the effect that, "…on 12 December 1967, the British Embassy was directed by London to further investigate the subject with a view to cooperating with the Russians in observation teams for UFOs." There may have been a very good reason for the actions of the Brits: between 1959 and1966, documentation now declassified by the British Ministry of Defense reveals, British authorities received a combined total of 446 UFO reports. In 1967, alone, however, the MoD was inundated with no less than 362 reports – averaging almost one report per day.

The DIA added that the Scientific Counselor of the British Embassy visited the Soviet Union's State Committee for Science and Technology and inquired about two things: (a) the status and nature of the Soviet UFO commission and; (b) the possibility of "British-Russian cooperation in observation of UFOs." According to the DIA's sources, "…the British counselor was politely received and the Commission was freely discussed. The British were told they would receive a reply to their request about cooperation."

DIA records reveal that the Brits did not receive a reply from the Soviets and "did not pursue the subject." But, the British Government *did* have its own opinions on the nature of the Soviet UFO program, however. The DIA documentation shows that, "The British Scientific Counselor believes that the original announcement of the work of the Commission on TV was an oversight on the part of the censors because the commission has not been reported or referred to anywhere else. Mr. [Censored] believes the Commission has not been disbanded, but will continue under cover. This information was sent to London."

Intriguingly, the DIA records also show that the relevant data had been provided by a source that had "read confidential British files on this subject." It is a pity that the DIA report – which was prepared by a Colonel Melvin J. Nielsen – did not expand upon the reference to these secret documents of the Brits. Nevertheless, that the British Government chose to make a stealthy approach to the Soviets – and directly in the wake of a significant wave of UFO activity in the skies of the UK – is more than notable. It suggests an undercurrent of concern and unease within certain British-based corridors of power.

Even though the Soviets chose not to take matters further with the Brits (and vice-versa), the very fact that the latter made the approach – *at all* – is notable. In 1991, I was informed in writing by the British Ministry of Defense that, with regard to UFOs, "…we do not co-operate with other Governments on this subject." That stance, however, did not seemingly prevent British authorities from at least *attempting* to work with the Soviets on the UFO problem – and practically a quarter of a century before I was assured there was *no* such cooperation at all!

Based upon what we have seen thus far, and how agencies of government have used the UFO phenomenon to dazzle and disturb potential enemies, I strongly suspect that the Brits were seeking to find a way to use the UFO phenomenon as a means to cause problems and worries for the Soviets. And vice-versa too. Time-wise, there is evidence that suggests this scenario is indeed the likely one. As we shall now see. It all revolves around a woman named Alice Bradley Sheldon.

To understand how and why the Brits – alongside their American counterparts – secretly decided to make use of the UFO phenomenon in the late 1960s, and for reasons relative to counterintelligence, disinformation programs, and Russian destabilization, we have to begin with a sensational saga that surfaced in November 2005. That was when a source using the term "Anonymous" came out of the shadows and told an incredible story. Some said it was *too* incredible to be true. It just might have been exactly that. It's a story surrounding what became known within Ufology as "The Serpo Documents." As for "Anonymous," he or she was said to have been a government insider with a wealth of information on some of the biggest UFO-themed secrets of all time. Here's what "Anonymous" shared with the UFO research community on the Serpo controversy:

> I am a retired employee of the U.S. Government. I won't go into any great details about my past, but I was involved in a special program. As for Roswell, it occurred, but not like the storybooks tell. There were two crash sites: one southwest of Corona, New Mexico and the second site at Pelona Peak, south of Datil, New Mexico.
>
> The crash involved two extraterrestrial aircraft. The Corona site was found a day later by an archaeological team. This team reported the crash site to the Lincoln County Sheriff's department. A deputy arrived the next day and summoned a state police officer. One live entity was found hiding behind a rock. The entity was given water but declined food. The entity was later transferred to Los Alamos.
>
> The information eventually went to Roswell Army Air Field. The site was examined and all evidence was removed. The bodies were taken to Los Alamos National

Laboratory because they had a freezing system that allowed the bodies to remain frozen for research. The craft was taken to Roswell and then onto Wright Field, Ohio.

The second site was not discovered until August 1949. Two ranchers found it. They reported their findings several days later to the sheriff of Catron County, New Mexico. Because of the remote location, it took the sheriff several days to make his way to the crash site. Once at the site, the sheriff took photographs and then drove back to Datil.

Sandia Army Base, Albuquerque, New Mexico was then notified. A recovery team from Sandia took custody of all evidence, including six bodies. The bodies were taken to Sandia Base, but later transferred to Los Alamos.

The live entity established communications with us and provided us with a location of his home planet. The entity remained alive until 1952, when he died. But before his death, he provided us with a full explanation of the items found inside the two crafts. One item was a communication device. The entity was allowed to make contact with his planet.

Somehow, I never knew this information, but a meeting date was set for April 1964 near Alamogordo, New Mexico. The Aliens landed and retrieved the bodies of their dead comrades. Information was exchanged. Communication was in English. The aliens had a translation device.

In 1965, we had an exchange program with the aliens. We carefully selected 12 military personnel; ten men and two women. They were trained, vetted and carefully removed from the military system. The 12 were skilled in various specialties.

Near the northern part of the Nevada Test Site, the aliens landed and the 12 Americans left. One entity was left on Earth. The original plan was for our 12 people to stay 10 years and then return to Earth.

But something went wrong. The 12 remained until 1978, when they were returned to the same location in Nevada. Seven men and one woman returned. Two died on the alien's home planet. Four others decided to remain, according to the returnees. Of the eight that returned, all have died. The last survivor died in 2002.

The returnees were isolated from 1978 until 1984 at various military installations. The Air Force Office of Special Investigations (AFOSI) was responsible for their security and safety. AFOSI also conducted debriefing sessions with the returnees.

That, basically, is the story of Serpo, which continues to circulate to this very day – although certainly not to the large extent that was seen in 2005. A few months after the story became widely known, an allegedly retired U.K. Ministry of Defense source came forward and shared certain data that suggested the Serpo story was not what it appeared to be. Using the alias of "Chapman," the highly talkative informant said the following of the statement from "Anonymous":

Interesting reading. However, these are NOT real events that are being described here, although the document they come from IS REAL. I saw this information in 1969 or '70 in Whitehall [London]. Originally it was a CIA document authored by a lady named Alice Bradley Sheldon. Its main purpose, if you will pardon the phrase, was to "scare the crap out of the Soviets" in response to them scaring the crap out of us. In the '60s, during the warmer part of the Cold War, the KGB successfully led the U.S. Government to believe that a number of nuclear devices had been concealed in disused mines and caves close to four (4) large American cities. These bombs could be detonated by sleeper agents at any time Moscow wished. It was not completely disproved that this was fake until 1980.

The "Project SERPO" report was part of the CIA's riposte to this and an attempt to trump the Soviets. Its aim was to make them believe that we had acquired lethal extraterrestrial energy devices and that we had a cozy friendship with these all-powerful EBENs [EBEN is allegedly a classified term used by American Intelligence to describe aliens. It is said to derive from the term "Extraterrestrial Biological Entity"] who would be very unhappy if Moscow attempted to harm the United States in any way. To a degree I believe this effort was effective to begin with.

However, it came unstuck when the CIA tried to over-reach the information by ADDING PHOTOGRAPHS and also trying to spook allies such as ourselves who were better equipped to analyze the information and bugged to the hilt by the KGB.

Why this information is being released again now I do not know. Possibly in the past the DIA could have BEEN FOOLED BY THE CIA into believing that "Project SERPO" was a real event and the ANONYMOUS source may genuinely want to release this information. Alternatively the DIA may have got it direct from the KGB most likely with a few choice modifications added by them.

It's most unfortunate that "Chapman" chose not to go public with a real name. There are, however, very good reasons as to why we *should* buy into the story of the Snowden-style informant. Alice Bradley Sheldon – who "Chapman" claimed wrote the Serpo papers decades ago – would certainly have been the ideal person to put just such a story together. Why so? Because she was both an employee of the CIA and a skillful writer of alien-themed science-fiction. A better person to employ – when it came to matters relative to both espionage and UFOs – it would have been hard to find. Let's take a look at the life and career of this fascinating character.

Alice Bradley was born in 1915 and, in the immediate aftermath of the horrific events that occurred at Pearl Harbor, Hawaii in December 1941, chose to do whatever she could for her government. It wasn't long before she was working in the heart of U.S. military intelligence. She ultimately rose to the rank of Major. In 1945, Alice Bradley became Alice Bradley Sheldon; that was the year in which she married Huntington D. Sheldon. The two decided to relocate to Washington D.C. and both accepted new and exciting careers in the CIA. Alice took part in espionage operations and worked on photo-analysis projects, such as studying imagery of Soviet military installations and then-new Russian aircraft. She remained with the CIA until 1955. As for Huntington, he rose to the position of the Director of the Office of Current Intelligence of the CIA. He held that same position until 1961.

In 1967, Alice decided to turn her hand to an area that she had a great love for: that of science-fiction. She did so, however, under the alias of James Tiptree, Jr. In 1973, a collection of her short stories hit the stands. It was entitled *Ten Thousand Light Years from Home*. Then, in 1975, *Warm World* and *Otherwise* were published to high acclaim. More books appeared: 1981's *Out of the Everywhere and Other Extraordinary Visions* and 1985's *Brightness Falls from the*

Air. Barely a handful of people knew, during her lifetime, that Alice and Tiptree were actually one and the very same.

The final years for Alice and her husband were sadly not good; not at all. Both were suffering from ill-health. Huntington finally became bed-ridden. The end was getting closer and closer. It finally arrived. On May 19, 1987, Alice shot and killed her sleeping husband, and then took her own life. Her secrets from that time spent in the employ of the CIA went with her. Unless there is a significant development in the matter of Alice Bradley Sheldon, the Serpo papers, and a plot designed to terrify the Russians, we may never get to see the full picture. But, I cannot think of a better, and more qualified, source than Sheldon –a sci-fi writer and a CIA employee – to whip up the saga of Serpo, as a means to freak out the Soviet Union.

It's eye-opening that "Chapman" claimed to have seen the Serpo files in 1969 or 1970. The reason? Nineteen-sixty-nine was the year in which an elaborate UFO-themed Soviet ruse was put into place. This one was highly sophisticated and revolved around a crashed UFO and the autopsy of an alleged alien creature. The story itself is undeniably fascinating – which is what the Russians were surely counting on – as the "evidence" is an old piece of film-footage that reportedly chronicled the whole thing. While the crash of the UFO is said to have occurred in March 1969, the story – and the attendant film – did not surface until 1998, almost three decades later. That was the year in which a television production, *The Secret KGB UFO Files*, was broadcast in the United States and elsewhere. A great deal of money was put into the over-sensationalized production and it was hosted by the late Roger Moore, the star of seven of the phenomenally successful *James Bond* movies. The documentary covered a wide body of UFO-based data (some of it blatantly hoaxed); however, there's no doubt that it was specifically the film of the supposed crashed UFO and its deceased crew-member which caught the attention of most of those who bothered to watch it.

Certainly, a great deal of effort went into the production of the film: this was no amateur, half-hearted operation. The footage is grainy, appears old, and was filmed by someone with a hand-held camera. It shows around fifteen-to-twenty men wearing Russian uniforms, thick coats and hats; they are all armed and are guarding a small, circular-shaped craft which appears to have slammed into the ground in a wooded, frosty area. The location was said to have been Sverdlovsky, Russia. The trees are largely bereft of leaves and everything points to the incident having occurred in very cold bleak weather. Only around a half of the saucer-shaped vehicle protrudes out of the soil, in an angled fashion. The inference is that the military unit found the craft shortly after it hit the ground and, at the time of the filming, were in the process of guarding the site from any and all onlookers that might have come along. To this day, we don't know where the film came from, and how it reached the producers of *The Secret KGB UFO Files*. We're told that the production company had to pay $10,000 U.S. dollars to secure it, after it was smuggled out of KGB archives. Supposedly.

It is worth noting the following from the National UFO Center: "The footage at the crash site does seem to be authentic at least on several points. The truck in the film is a circa 1950 model ZIS151, which has not been used by the military for quite some time, and the truck would have been difficult to find to stage a hoax with. Other elements of the film do not exhibit any obvious signs of a hoax." It should be noted there are two other, old military vehicles in the film, too.

As for the remaining portion of the film, it very much mirrors the notorious "Alien Autopsy" film, which, in 1995, was foisted on the world by a man named Ray Santilli, and to wildly

⌐ of fanfare. Three men appear to be working ⌐psy of a small, humanoid creature, while a woman ⌐tes. Numerous websites claim that the woman has been ⌐tified as a "KGB stenographer" named "O.A. Pshonikina." This statement has been repeated time and again, yet there is no evidence to prove the claim. Such is the reliability – or not - of the Internet.

Did this footage amount to the Soviet Union's hasty response to the Serpo operation? To have the U.S. Government and the intelligence community to think that the Russians had recovered, and were extensively studying, alien creatures and their technology? These are mind-boggling, yet utterly plausible, questions to ponder on.

14.

"THE JOVIETJ AND THE KGB WERE UJING U.J. CITIZENJ AND UFO GROUPJ"

December 11, 1984 was a date destined to become infamous in the field of Ufology. On that day, a man named Jaime Shandera, who was a television producer at the time, received in the mail a thick, manila envelope. It was postmarked Albuquerque, New Mexico and lacked a return address. Greg Bishop says that "two more envelopes were inside, each enclosed within the next like Russian dolls." As will soon become apparent, Bishop's Russian analogy proves to be a highly apt one. It still is. Bishop added: "From the third one, a 35mm roll of film rolled out of a black canister. When developed, the black-and-white film revealed two sequences of eight pictures each – pictures of something that would pass into history as the notorious 'MJ-12 document' or 'Presidential Briefing Papers.'" They appeared to be nothing less than decades-old, highly-classified papers on a Top Secret program of the U.S. Government. Those same papers revolved around crashed saucers, dead aliens, autopsies of extraterrestrial creatures, and a secret agency or think-tank – maybe even a full-on cabal – known as Majestic 12.

In 1984, Shandera was working with William L. "Bill" Moore, the co-author with Charles Berlitz of two controversial books: 1979's *The Philadelphia Experiment* and *The Roswell Incident*, which was published in the following year. The former told the sensational story of an attempt to make a U.S. Navy ship invisible in 1943, while the latter was focused on the saga of an alleged crashed UFO in New Mexico in the late 1940s. Back in the mid-seventies, when Moore's research into the Roswell affair was taking off, the case was nowhere near being the forever-growing colossus which it certainly is to this very day. In fact, in the post-1947 period, the event had practically been forgotten or dismissed by the UFO research field - lost to the fog of time after a brief, manic period of notoriety in early July 1947. Moore's work, alongside that of UFO investigator Stanton Friedman, served to reignite the cold coals of Roswell. They would soon be scalding hot. It was this resurrection of the story of Roswell that ultimately led Moore, in particular, to find himself plunged into a world filled with what are colloquially known as secret agents, spies, and government spooks. This Machiavellian group worked hard to come across to Moore as comrades in arms; benevolent combinations of the NSA's Edward Snowden and Watergate's Deep-Throat, Mark Felt. They were willing to share with Moore what they claimed were some of the U.S. Government's most guarded UFO secrets. In return for allowing Moore a tantalizing peek behind the curtains, one might suggest, they insisted that, in return, Moore had to do something for them. It wasn't particularly savory; Faustian pacts very seldom are. If ever, even. We'll come back, shortly, to the matter of the dark deal that was placed on the table for Moore.

There's no doubt that *something* crashed to earth on the Foster Ranch, Lincoln County, New Mexico at some point around Independence Day 1947. The big question that still stands to this day is: what was it? It's a fact that after being appraised of the situation at the ranch by the local sheriff's office, military personnel from the Roswell Army Air Field headed out to see what all of the fuss and palaver was about. Depending on whose version of events you accept as being real – the Air Force, the Government Accountability Office, or numerous ufologists - those on the scene stumbled on a wrecked spacecraft from another world, a weather-balloon, a "secret balloon" designed to monitor for early Soviet atomic bomb tests, a Russian aircraft, a time-machine from the future, or a rocket filled with a crew of shaved chimpanzees. And, that's just the start. Today, the number of theories for what happened approximately an hour's drive from Roswell has reached no less than *fifteen*. By the time you finish reading this book it may very well be sixteen; I would not be surprised.

When portions of the wreckage were retrieved by the military, staff at the old and long-closed-down Roswell Army Air Field announced that they had recovered the remains of what was termed in a press-release as a "flying disc." It was a statement that caught the attention of many. How could it not? Even the U.K.'s *Times* newspaper sat up and took notice of that one, as did the Hong Kong press. Twenty-four hours later, though, the sensational story was utterly crushed to pulp: "Sorry, guys," said the Army Air Force, "No flying disc, after all. Just a weather-balloon." The press moved onto new stories and soon forgot about the strange, potentially unearthly incident. The legend of the doomed little men from the stars, however - their bodies said to have been found decaying quickly under the hot, baking sun of New Mexico, and their ship torn to pieces, so the story goes – would resurface years later, thanks to Moore and Friedman.

While still a team at the time – they ultimately parted ways in the 1980s - the pair chased down old-timers from the military, locals in the Roswell area who remembered all too well the weird events that went on in July 1947, and just about anyone and every-one with something of significance to say on the matter. Soon, there would be enough material to present a reasonably-sized manuscript to a publisher, which is exactly what happened. Moore and Berlitz's 1980 book, *The Roswell Incident*, makes for intriguing reading, but it's most certainly padded out: it contains wholly irrelevant material on UFO sightings reported by U.S. astronauts, for example, as well as overseas UFO encounters that have zero bearing on Roswell.

Moore and Friedman continued to enthusiastically work on the case. Berlitz, meanwhile, turned his attentions elsewhere, such as trying to find the location of Noah's Ark and delving into prophecies of worldwide Armageddon in 1999 (it didn't happen, folks). It became clear fairly quickly that there was one big problem for Moore: despite the in-depth investigations, the publication of the book, and more than a few potentially significant leads suggesting that the weather-balloon scenario was an undeniable lie, Moore knew he was facing an almost impenetrable brick-wall. Those who *really* knew what happened, and saw the bodies - such as Bill Rickett and Sheridan Cavitt, both of the old Counter-Intelligence Corps, and both at Roswell in 1947 – were saying next to nothing. Both men were fearful of unleashing an old dark secret they had pledged would never be revealed. What was needed was a break in the story. It soon came. But, was it the real thing? Or, was Moore himself about to find himself subjected to carefully directed deception?

In September 1980, while promoting *The Roswell Incident*, Moore took part in a number of radio-based interviews around the United States. At the end of one such interview, a secretary told Moore that there was someone on the line who wanted to speak privately with Moore. The voice at the other end belonged to a colonel who was stationed at Offutt Air Force Base, which is located in Sarpy County, Nebraska. The man said to Moore, as Greg Bishop tells it in his 2005 book, *Project Beta*: "We think you're the only one we've heard that seems to know what he's talking about." The colonel desired a meeting. And soon, too. Moore scribbled down the colonel's number, promising to get back in touch as soon as possible. The proactive colonel didn't wait for Moore to reach him, however. Instead, he contacted Moore – for a second time. Once again, the man trotted out those same sixteen words: "We think you're the only one we've heard that seems to know what he's talking about." By now, Moore was more than intrigued. A meeting was quickly arranged. The pair was to rendezvous in an Albuquerque restaurant, one that was on Moore's journey home, for good food and – hopefully - enlightening conversation. The mysterious informant was described by Moore as being elderly and gaunt. Greg Bishop said that the man had a "hint of an Eastern European accent." From that day on, the wizened old man would become known to Moore as "The Falcon."

Greg Bishop says that, "…[Moore's] new acquaintance told [him] that he represented a group of intelligence agents in the U.S. Government who were tired of the secrecy surrounding the UFO subject and were eager to release more accurate information to the public. They wanted to do this through a reputable researcher. He would be given small bites of the story over time, and could do with it as he wished. Would Moore be interested in participating in such a program?"

Yes, Moore *was* interested. *Very much so*. But, there was the matter of that aforementioned unholy alliance, which Moore knew he would have to enter into; like it or not. He knew that if he didn't play the game, then his chance of getting to the heart of what Uncle Sam knew of UFOs and aliens – dead, alive or even both - would irreversibly slip out of his grip. So, Moore agreed to do whatever had to be done. And fuck the cost. Maybe, even the consequences, too. Everything soon took off: in the early 1980s, Moore found himself periodically on the receiving end of instructions to travel to certain locations around the United States, where he would meet with anonymous, insider-type characters, including, yet again, the Falcon.

On each occasion seemingly highly-classified material on UFOs was handed over to Moore – always in manila envelopes and in various widespread places. Those locations included a motel-room in upstate New York and a certain building in the heart of Los Angeles, California. On one occasion, in April 1983, a friend of Moore's, Nic Magnuson, picked up a collection of documents for Moore at Seattle, Washington's Sea-Tac International Airport. The handover was made by "a short, elderly, balding man" who gave Magnuson a newspaper that contained hidden within its pages one of those priceless manila envelopes. The collective documentation referred to such enigmas as "Project Aquarius," "MJ12 [an alternative term for Majestic 12]," "communications with aliens," even to decisions taken by elite figures in the domain of intelligence-gathering to keep the White House firmly out of the ufological loop. A secret that was so astounding that not even the president of the United States could be told the truth? Possibly, yes.

For Moore there was very little doubt the papers amounted to absolute dynamite. If they were true, that is. That was the biggest issue of all: *were* they genuine? Or, was Moore being used by people in the intelligence community; manipulative characters who were trying to push Moore away from his genuinely significant Roswell research and further down a pathway filled with questionable document upon questionable document? And, still hanging over Moore's head like the sword of Damocles, there was that part of the deal that Moore had to fulfil if he was to continue to receive regular supplies of those seemingly priceless papers. Moore's part in all of this revolved around a man named Paul Bennewitz.

An Albuquerque, New Mexico physicist who died in 2003, Paul Bennewitz spent a significant amount of time digging into U.S. Air Force- and National Security Agency-based top secret projects which, from the late-seventies to the early-eighties, were housed at Kirtland Air Force Base, New Mexico. Bennewitz believed those projects were connected to the activities of sinister extraterrestrials. They soared across the skies above Kirtland AFB by star-filled, moonlit nights, demonstrating their extraterrestrial invulnerability and power. It's hardly surprising that, for years, Bennewitz was under deep surveillance by the U.S. military and a number of intelligence services. He was, as a consequence of his digging, bombarded by the murky world of officialdom with a mass of disinformation, faked stories, and outright lies in order to divert him from his research. It worked. In fact, and to Bennewitz's eternal cost, it worked just *too* damned well. By the mid-eighties, he was heading for complete mental disintegration.

The intelligence community cared not a bit that Bennewitz thought their secret operations were UFO-related – precisely because the UFO connection was one of Bennewitz's very own making. There *was*, however, deep concern on the part of the world of officialdom that by digging into classified activities at Kirtland in search of UFOs, Bennewitz just might inadvertently reveal – *to the spies of the Soviet Union, in a worst-case scenario* – information and technology that had to be kept secret at all costs, even if those costs included Bennewitz's own sanity and health. Which, ultimately, they did. And, so, a grim plan was initiated.

U.S. agents learned the essential parts of Bennewitz's theories from the man himself, by actually breaking into his home while he was out and checking his files and research notes. Bennewitz's beliefs were astounding and controversial: aliens were mutilating cattle as part of some weird genetic experiment. The E.T.s were abducting American citizens and implanting them with small devices for purposes disturbingly unknown. Those same aliens were living deep underground in a secure fortress below the Archuleta Mesa at Dulce, New Mexico. And everyone was soon going to be in deep and dire trouble as a direct result of the presence of this brewing, intergalactic threat. So the Air Force gave Bennewitz precisely what he was looking for: confirmation that his theories were all true, and more. This was, however, all just a carefully-planned ruse to bombard Bennewitz with so much faked UFO data in the hope that it would steer him away from the classified military projects of a non-UFO nature that he had uncovered. And, sure enough, it all worked very well. For the government. Far less so for Bennewitz.

When Bennewitz received conformation (albeit carefully controlled and utterly fabricated confirmation) that, yes, he had stumbled upon the horrible truth and that, yes, there really was an alien base deep below Dulce, the actions of the Intelligence community had the desired effect: Bennewitz became increasingly paranoid and unstable, and he began looking away from Kirtland (the hub of the down-to-earth secrets of the NSA and the Air Force that had to be kept) and harmlessly towards the vicinity of Dulce, where his actions, research, and theories could be carefully controlled and manipulated by the government. At this time American Intelligence brought Bill Moore into the secret scheme and asked him to keep them informed of how well – from their perspective - the disinformation operations against Bennewitz were working. In return, Moore was promised – and provided with – data and documents on super-secret, official UFO projects, crashed saucers, dead aliens, and more. That, then, was the nature of the bleak agreement between Moore and the man with the European accent, the Falcon.

All of which brings us to what happened after December 11, 1984, the date on which Jaime Shandera received the ever-controversial Majestic 12 documents. It's a story as mind-blowing as that of Paul Bennewitz – partly because it was interconnected, as we shall further see. It caused the FBI's counterintelligence staff to suspect that those same documents were the creations of no less than disinformation agents of the Russian government.

In the summer of 1987, Sidgwick & Jackson published Timothy Good's book, *Above Top Secret: The Worldwide UFO Cover-Up*. It contained copies of the same controversial Majestic 12 documents that had been dropped through Jaime Shandera's mailbox some three years earlier. According to Good, he got his copies of the pages in March 1987 from "a CIA source." Good has been consistently cagey when it comes to the matter of how, precisely, he obtained his copies of the files. And from whom, too. Two months after Good's CIA insider provided him with the documents, the London *Observer* newspaper mentioned the Majestic 12 documents. The date of the article was May 31, 1987. Written by Martin Bailey it had the lengthy title of "Close encounters of an alien kind – and now if you've read enough about the election, here's news from another world."

In no time, Moore, Shandera and Friedman chose to release *their* copies into the public domain, which is hardly surprising, given the fact that word of the Majestic 12 papers was now starting to trickle and circulate outside of the confines of the trio. This was completely understandable: after all, the three had done all of the groundwork, and the very last thing they wanted was to be written out of the story – or, at the absolute least, left marginalized and sitting frustratingly on the sidelines.

As an aside, Alice Bradley Sheldon, who very likely wrote the "Serpo" papers back in the late 1960s, killed herself and her husband less than two weeks before the Majestic 12 documents mailed to Jaime Shandera were first publicly referenced – namely, in the pages of the London *Observer* newspaper. Also, James Jesus Angleton, who was the Chief of CIA Counterintelligence operations from 1954 to 1975, and who was rumored to have been "in the know" when it came to Majestic 12, died in that very same month. Lung-cancer took him on May 11 at the age of sixty-nine.

When it comes to the content of the Majestic 12 material, what we have is a document which purports to be a 1952 briefing prepared by Admiral Roscoe H. Hillenkoetter for President-elect Dwight D. Eisenhower, informing him that a spacecraft from another world, along with a number of alien bodies, had been recovered from the New Mexico desert in 1947. A second document is a 1947 memorandum from President Harry Truman to Secretary of Defense James Forrestal, authorizing the establishment of the Majestic 12 group. For years – in fact, for decades – UFO sleuths have argued on the matter of the documents' authenticity or otherwise. It's no surprise that ufologists still can't come to a consensus that satisfies everyone. Such is the nature of the domain of UFO research.

In 1990, Moore and Shandera published a highly detailed, 111-pages-long "analytical report" on the Majestic 12 documents. It revealed a great deal of documentation that had hitherto remained hidden from the UFO research community. With regards to their forensic study of the Eisenhower Briefing Document, the pair stated that: "This very controversial document has held up well under an intense effort to examine all aspects of it…" On the matter of the Truman memo, they admitted that "…the case for the document stands on somewhat weaker ground than the case for the companion Eisenhower document." Overall, the pair concluded that, "…as for the document as a whole, it is either authentic or a well done and very probably official fabrication.

We give a value of 35-40% for the former possibility, and 60-65% for the latter."

The late Philip Coppens, who followed the UFO controversy deeply, said of the Majestic 12 controversy that, "…the stakes were high and if the documents were genuine, it was indeed the smoking gun UFOlogy had been searching for over the past four decades. Hence, the Fund for UFO Research (FUFOR), headed by US Navy physicist Dr. Bruce Maccabee, paid researcher Stanton Friedman $16,000 to investigate the initial MJ-12 documents."

We'll soon return to Maccabee, and a strange encounter he had with a Russian official in the post-Majestic 12 era.

Philip Klass, right up until the time of his passing in 2005, was the arch enemy of the UFO research community of the 1960s to the mid-2000s; he was a man who never came across a UFO case he couldn't solve (in his own mind, at least). Perhaps best known for his long-time writings for *Aviation Week & Space Technology* - one of the most respected, regular publications dedicated to all things of the aerospace kind - he also spent a decade in the employ of General Electric. Bill Moore had no love for Klass. The feeling was definitively mutual. So, when the Majestic 12 documents appeared publicly, and Klass realized that it was Moore who appeared to be the key figure in the saga of MJ12, he, Klass, chose to take swift and controversial action. Renowned for his mean streak, and his "hell hath no fury like a woman scorned"-type demeanor, Klass made no qualms at all about suggesting that Moore himself had created the documents. Klass decided to write to the FBI and tell them what was afoot in saucer land: either highly-classified documents were circulating among who-knew-how-many ufologists, or the whole thing was a huge, grand hoax of epic proportions. Whichever scenario was the correct one, Klass suggested that the FBI needed to take a look at what was going down and figure it all out. Klass chose to pen his letter to William Baker, who, at the time, was the Assistant Director in the Office of Congressional and Public Affairs.

Jacques Vallee - the author of a number of groundbreaking UFO-themed books, such as *Passport to Magonia* and *Messengers of Deception* - and a former principal investigator on Department of Defense computer networking projects - stated in his 1991 book *Revelations* that the FBI turned away from the Majestic 12 documents in "disgust" and professed no interest in the matter. That's not exactly how it happened, though; far from it. So far as can be determined, when the FBI got deeply involved in the matter of the murky documents and their unclear origins, one investigation – says journalist and author Howard Blum - was undertaken by Special Agent Nicholas Boone (in Los Angeles) and a second one by Special Agent William Zinnikas (in Manhattan). Today, Zinnikas is a private consultant on counterterrorism and security issues. Boone is a successful screenwriter.

As I noted in my self-published paper, *MJ-12 – The FBI Connection*: the aforementioned Howard Blum - a *New York Times* bestselling author of such very well-received books as *Gangland* and *Wanted!* – spent a great deal of time investigating the matter of the Majestic 12 papers in the late 1980s. While researching and writing his 1990 UFO-themed book, *Out There*, Blum did his utmost to solve the riddle of flying saucers. He soon learned - just like so many UFO researchers over the years have – that solving just about *anything* in the domain of UFOs was no easy feat. Blum has stated that of those who were approached by the FBI in the latter part of 1988, one was a "Working Group" established under the auspices of the Defense Intelligence Agency, and which was tasked with looking at the UFO problem.

In 1990, Blum was interviewed by the now-defunct *UFO Magazine* and was asked if the Working Group could have been a "front" for another, even more covert, investigative body within the heart of the U.S. government. Maybe, something like Majestic 12. Blum's response aptly sums up one of the major problems faced by both those inside and outside of government when trying to determine exactly who knows what in relation to the Majestic 12 controversy:

"Interestingly," said Blum to the staff of *UFO Magazine*, "members of [the Working Group] aired that possibility themselves. When looking into the MJ12 papers, some members of the group said - and not in jest: "Perhaps we're just a front organization for some sort of MJ12. Suppose, in effect, we conclude the MJ12 papers are phony, are counterfeit. Then we've solved the entire mystery for the government, relieving them of the burden in dealing with it, and at the same time, we allow the real secret to remain held by a higher source. An FBI agent told me there are so many secret levels within the government that even the government isn't aware of it!"

As I also said in *MJ-12 – The FBI Connection*: We also know that what was possibly *yet another* fall 1988 investigation was conducted by the FBI's Foreign Counter-Intelligence division. Some input into the investigation also came from the FBI office in Dallas, Texas; the involvement of the latter was confirmed to me by Oliver "Buck" Revell, a now-retired Special Agent in Charge of Dallas, Texas' FBI office. On September 15, 1988, an agent of the Air Force Office of Special Investigations contacted Dallas FBI and supplied the Bureau with a copy of the Majestic 12 papers. This set was obtained from a source whose identity, according to documentation released to me by the Bureau, the AFOSI has deemed must remain classified to this day. On October 25, 1988, the Dallas office transmitted a two-page Secret Airtel to headquarters that read as follows:

> Enclosed for the Bureau is an envelope that contains a possible classified document. Dallas notes that within the last six weeks, there has been local publicity regarding "OPERATION MAJESTIC-12" with at least two appearances on a local radio talk show, discussing the MAJESTIC-12 OPERATION, the individuals involved, and the Government's attempt to keep it all secret. It is unknown if this is all part of a publicity campaign. [Censored] from OSI, advises that "OPERATION BLUE BOOK," mentioned in the document on page 4 did exist. Dallas realizes that the purported document is over 35 years-old, but does not know if it has been properly declassified. The Bureau is requested to discern if the document is still classified. Dallas will hold any investigation in abeyance until further direction from FBIHQ.

Partly due of the actions of the Dallas FBI Office, and partly as a result of the investigation undertaken by the FBI's Foreign Counter-Intelligence staff, on November 30, 1988, an arranged meeting took place in Washington D.C. between agents of the Bureau and those of the AFOSI. If the AFOSI had information on Majestic 12, said the Bureau, they would definitely like to know. And, quickly please. A Secret communication back to the Dallas office from Washington on December 2, 1988 read: "This communication is classified Secret in its entirety. Reference Dallas Airtel dated October 25 1988. Reference Airtel requested that FBIHQ determine if the document enclosed by referenced

Airtel was classified or not. The Office of Special Investigations, US Air Force, advised on November 30, 1988, that the document was fabricated. Copies of that document have been distributed to various parts of the United States. The document is completely bogus. Dallas is to close captioned investigation."

At first glance, that would seem to lay matters to rest once and for all. Unfortunately, it does not. It only serves to make things even more confusing and mysterious.

Also in *MJ-12 – The FBI Connection*, I said: there's no doubt that the Air Force played a most strange game with respect to the Majestic 12 documents. The FBI was assured by the AFOSI that the papers were fabricated; however, Special Agent Frank Batten, Jr., chief of the Information Release Division at the Investigative Operations Center with the USAF, confirmed to me that AFOSI has never maintained any records pertaining to either Majestic 12, or any investigation thereof. This begs an important question: how was the AFOSI able to determine that the papers were faked if no investigation on their part was undertaken? Batten also advised me that while the AFOSI did "discuss" the Majestic 12 documents with the FBI, they made absolutely no written reference to that meeting in any shape or form. This is most odd and unusual: government and military agencies are methodical when it comes to documenting possible breaches of security. Arguably, this case should have been no different. Apparently, though, *it was*.

Richard L. Weaver, formerly the Deputy for Security and Investigative Programs with the U.S. Air Force (and the author of the U.S. Air Force's 1995 near-1000 page, mega-sized report, *The Roswell Report: Fact Vs. Fiction in the New Mexico Desert*), advised me similarly on October 12, 1993: "The Air Force considers the MJ12 (both the group described and the purported documents to be bogus." Weaver, too, conceded, however, that there were "no documents responsive" to my request for Air Force files on how just such a determination was reached. Stanton Friedman also stated that, based on his correspondence with Weaver on the issue of Majestic 12, he, too, was dissatisfied with the responses that he received after filing similar FOIA requests relating to the way in which the Air Force made its "bogus" determination. Moreover, there is the fact that AFOSI informed the FBI that, "copies of that document have been distributed to various parts of the United States." To make such a statement AFOSI simply must have conducted at least *some* form of investigation or have been in receipt of data from yet another agency. On the other hand, if AFOSI truly did not undertake any such investigation into Majestic 12, then its statement to the FBI decrying the value of the documents is essentially worthless, since it is based on personal opinion rather than sound evaluation.

We aren't quite done with Majestic 12 and the FBI. It's now time to take a look at an astounding theory that one arm of the FBI – the Foreign Counterintelligence division – addressed: that the Majestic 12 papers were the work of the Soviets. But, just before we do that, let's see how and why counterintelligence is such a vital component of the important work of the special-agents of the FBI. In the Bureau's own words:

> Spies might seem like a throwback to earlier days of world wars and cold wars, but they are more prolific than ever—and they are targeting our nation's most valuable secrets. The threat is not just the more traditional spies passing U.S. secrets to foreign governments, either to make money or advance their ideological agendas. It is also students and scientists and plenty of others stealing the valuable trade secrets of American universities and

businesses—the ingenuity that drives our economy—and providing them to other countries. It is nefarious actors sending controlled technologies overseas that help build bombs and weapons of mass destruction designed to hurt and kill Americans and others. Because much of today's spying is accomplished by data theft from computer networks, espionage is quickly becoming cyber-based.

The FBI has been responsible for identifying and neutralizing ongoing national security threats from foreign intelligence services since 1917, nine years after the Bureau was created in 1908. The FBI's Counterintelligence Division, which is housed within the National Security Branch, has gone through a lot of changes over the years, and throughout the Cold War the division changed its name several times. But foiling and countering the efforts of the Soviet Union and other communist nations remained the primary mission.

While the Counterintelligence Division continues to neutralize national security threats from foreign intelligence services, its modern-day mission is much broader. The FBI is the lead agency for exposing, preventing, and investigating intelligence activities on U.S. soil, and the Counterintelligence Division uses its full suite of investigative and intelligence capabilities to combat counterintelligence threats. While the details of the FBI's strategy are classified, the overall goals are as follows:

*Protect the secrets of the U.S. Intelligence Community, using intelligence to focus investigative efforts, and collaborating with our government partners to reduce the risk of espionage and insider threats.

*Protect the nation's critical assets, like our advanced technologies and sensitive information in the defense, intelligence, economic, financial, public health, and science and technology sectors.

*Counter the activities of foreign spies. Through proactive investigations, the Bureau identifies who they are and stops what they're doing.

*Keep weapons of mass destruction from falling into the wrong hands, and use intelligence to drive the FBI's investigative efforts to keep threats from becoming reality.

All of which brings us back to Majestic 12 and the FBI.

FBI agents attached to the Foreign Counterintelligence division came up with three theories to try and solve the riddle of the Majestic 12 papers: (a) that they were the work of the likes of the Falcon and his equally shadowy cohorts in the Paul Bennewitz saga; (b) that they were the creations of a think-tank within the Defense Intelligence Agency, which had fabricated them as a means to divert UFO investigators from a *real* Majestic 12-type group; and (c) *that they had been put together by Soviet disinformation experts.* Howard Blum states that the FBI's reasoning for suspecting the Russians were at the heart of the Majestic 12 affair revolved around "muddying the waters, creating dissension, spreading paranoia in the ranks – those were all the day-in, day-out jobs of the ruthless operation." Revenge against U.S. Intelligence – for having spun their own UFO-themed operations against Russia in earlier years and decades – was also seen as a distinct possibility.

Directly connected to the Soviet theory is the fact that, as U.S. Intelligence learned to its consternation during both the 1970s and the 1980s, an unclear number of unnamed UFO researchers, with important links to the U.S. defense industry, had been compromised by Soviet agents. It went like this: those saucer-seekers who worked in the field of defense, and who had been caught tightly in a Kremlin web, would secretly provide the Russians with top secret data on the likes of the F-117 *Nighthawk* "stealth fighter" and the B-2 *Spirit* "stealth bomber" - which, at the time, were still highly classified and in test-stage out at the likes of the notorious Area 51. In return, the KGB would provide those same American researchers with sensational documents on crashed UFOs and dead aliens. The plan that Moscow had in mind was for the Russians to get their eager hands on *real* top secret U.S. documents that could be used to advance Russian military aviation programs; but those hapless UFO investigators would receive nothing but *faked* garbage from their Soviet handlers, such as – you've got it - the Majestic 12 documents. This very much echoes the concerns that Australia's intelligence agency, the ASIO, had about pilot Ricky Royal years earlier, in the late-1950s. It's important to note there *is* evidence to support this 1970s/1980s "dangling carrot" theory, in relation to the Majestic 12 documents and the Russians, as we'll now see.

In 1999, Gerald K. Haines – in his position as the historian of the National Reconnaissance Office - wrote a paper titled "CIA's Role in the Study of UFOs, 1947-90." It's now in the public domain, thanks to the provisions of the Freedom of Information Act. It can be read at the CIA's website. Haines' paper detailed the history of how, and why, the CIA became interested and involved in the phenomenon of UFOs. Although Haines covered a period of more than forty years, I will bring your attention to one particular section of his paper, which is focused on the 1970s-1980s. Haines wrote: "During the late 1970s and 1980s, the Agency continued its low-key interest in UFOs and UFO sightings. While most scientists now dismissed flying saucers reports as a quaint part of the 1950s and 1960s, some in the Agency and in the Intelligence Community shifted their interest to studying parapsychology and psychic phenomena associated with UFO sightings. CIA officials also looked at the UFO problem to determine what UFO sightings might tell them about Soviet progress in rockets and missiles and reviewed its counterintelligence aspects."

The Soviets, then, were camouflaging their secret rocket tests by spreading false and fantastic tales of UFOs. Haines also noted something that is absolutely key to the story that this book tells and particularly so with regard to the Majestic 12 papers: "Agency analysts from the Life Science Division of OSI and OSWR officially devoted a small amount of their time to issues relating to UFOs. *These included counterintelligence concerns that the Soviets and the KGB were using U.S. citizens and UFO groups to obtain information on sensitive U.S. weapons development programs (such as the Stealth aircraft), the vulnerability of the U.S. air-defense network to penetration by foreign missiles mimicking UFOs, and evidence of Soviet advanced technology associated with UFO sightings* [italics mine]."

What about those "U.S. citizens" that Haines referred to? Let us see.

The 1970s and 1980s were the decades in which Paul Bennewitz was most active, at least in terms of his UFO research in and around Kirtland Air Force Base, Albuquerque, New Mexico. He was almost certainly one of those Americans who Haines was talking about and whose actions the CIA's counterintelligence people were worried about. That the U.S. Air Force was very concerned by the possibility that Bennewitz was unknowingly being used by the Soviets; that was reason enough alone to practically force-feed Bennewitz with almost unending, nightmarish horror stories of dangerous and deadly aliens under Dulce, New Mexico. And then, have Bill Moore report back on the extent that those same horror stories were destabilizing Bennewitz's increasingly paranoid mind. All of this strongly suggests that Moore may have been as much a victim as Bennewitz was: both men may have been fed wholly bogus material. Interestingly, Haines actually references Shandera and Moore's work on the Majestic 12 documents in the "Notes" section of his very own paper.

A final aspect on this particular part of the story: Maybe Moore *was* used, but not by U.S. intelligence. Let's not forget that, as Greg Bishop noted, the Falcon had what was described as an eastern European accent. He may well not have been an American, which suggests the incredible theory that the Russians may have been running the program to learn all they could from Bennewitz. Or, maybe, there was *more than one Falcon*, which really serves to complicate matters.

Based on private data provided to him by sources in the know, Greg Bishop has concluded that the Falcon was probably a man named Harry Rositzke; he ran covert programs for the CIA, after cutting his teeth in the heart of the Second World War-era Office of Strategic Services. Rositzke, a Brooklyn native, was an expert on the matter of Soviet intelligence, the KGB, and Russia's programs designed to destabilize the West with carefully crafted propaganda. Rositzke, who died in 2002 at the age of ninety-one, wrote a number of non-fiction books on the world of espionage, including *The KGB: The Eyes of Russia* and *The CIA's Secret Operations*. Rositzke, it's important to note, did not have a European accent. That revelation adds further weight to the possibility that there may have been competing Falcons; one, Rositzke, an American trying to protect U.S. government secrets. The other? An unknown European character posing as an American official, and using the same alias of the Falcon, and trying to further disrupt U.S. intelligence.

When the story of Majestic 12 got more and more complicated and multi-layered, Bill Moore quite reasonably tried to get his hands on his FBI file – if such a thing existed. It turns out that such a thing *did* exist. It has to be said that it would have been a huge surprise if there *wasn't* such a file on Moore, given all that had gone down with regard to crashed UFOs, bodies of aliens on ice, the FBI connection, and allegedly leaked top secret papers on extraterrestrial life. On November 16, 1988 – when the FBI's investigation of the Majestic 12 papers was at its height – UFO investigator Larry Bryant sent a letter to one Hope Nakamura; she worked for the Center for National Security Studies. Bryant explained to Nakamura that Moore was looking to try and obtain his FBI file and determine what it contained. There was a good reason for this: Moore had already been able to determine that a file existed on him, which ran close to sixty pages; but he was having trouble getting the papers declassified. Moore's file got lengthier when the FBI's Majestic 12 probe got ever more complicated, which is hardly a surprise. Notably, some of the documents on Moore, the man himself learned, fell under the "B1" category of the Freedom of Information Act. Rather notably, B1 covers U.S. national security issues. This was quite a revelation. For Moore, though, not necessarily a good one.

In a proactive fashion, and with regard to Moore's file, Bryant put together an ad for publication in various military-themed publications. The ad was titled "UFO Secrecy/Congress-Watch." Among its highlights, it revealed that Moore's FBI was officially classed at a "Secret" level, and it demonstrated that *another* agency, beyond the FBI, was also watching Moore. The ad was published on November 23, 1988, in *The Pentagram*, an official U.S. Army publication. Bryant, in the ad, suggested that those reading it should demand a congressional hearing in relation to the UFO phenomenon. Despite Bryan's gung-ho approach, and help and advice from the Center for National Security Studies, Moore only managed to secure a small portion of his file.

One year later, 1989, Bryant tried to get a hold of any and all files that the FBI might have had on yet another figure in the Majestic 12 story: Stanton Friedman. The FBI got back to Bryant on August 2: "Mr. Friedman is the subject of one Headquarters main file. This file is classified in its entirety and I am affirming the denial of access to it." Attempts to determine the length and the scope of the file fell flat. So, on August 28, Bryant filed a suit in the District Court for the Eastern District of Columbia. He said: "My complaint seeks full disclosure of the UFO-related content of the FBI dossier on Stan Friedman. Neither Stan nor I have been able to convince the U.S. Federal Bureau of Investigation to loosen its grasp on that dossier, which Bureau officials assert, bears a security classification."

A few, scant pages were all that the FBI was willing to give up. Not much has changed since.

If the FBI learned anything further about Majestic 12 in the post-1989 period, then that information has not surfaced under the terms of the Freedom of Information Act. We *do* know something of deep interest though, thanks to a man named Richard L. Huff. He served as Bureau Co-Director within the Office of Information and Privacy. In correspondence (specifically on July 22, 1993), Huff informed me of the existence of an FBI "Main File" on Majestic 12, which is now in what is termed "closed status." The title of the file is not something along the lines of "Potentially leaked document" or "Questionable document," as one might imagine, given the strange story detailed in this chapter. Rather, the file title is nothing less than – wait for it – "*Espionage*." While we're admittedly forced to speculate, that one, eye-opening word alone strongly suggests that the Majestic 12 saga really *did* revolve around those very same components that surface in the pages of this chapter: spies, counterintelligence operations, the Moore-Bennewitz situation, the words of Gerald K. Haines, and the interference of the Russians. *And espionage*. There is another thing that adds further weight to this argument.

You'll recall that the Fund for UFO Research funded Stanton Friedman to the tune of a hefty sixteen grand to investigate the controversial Majestic 12 papers. Keep that in mind when you read the following words of Maccabee himself, which might suggest an ongoing monitoring by the Russians – and by U.S. intelligence, too - of the key figures in the Majestic 12 caper: "After I spoke at a UFO conference near Washington, D.C. in February 1993, *I was contacted by an assistant military attaché who was stationed at the Russian Embassy* [italics mine]. He wanted to know how to obtain U.S. government files on UFOs. You can imagine my surprise and amusement when, about six months later, while I was at work I got a call from the 'dreaded' FBI. It became obvious to me that the agent didn't know much about the UFO phenomenon and was amused to learn about the FBI files on the subject. *But he was especially interested in my interactions with the military attaché* [italics mine]."

In 2014, there was yet *another* development in the controversy surrounding Majestic 12: the Department of Defense declassified a previously top secret file on what was known during the Cold War as Project Pandora. To a significant degree, the program was focused on Cold War secrets of the Russians, and how microwaves can affect the mind and body to dangerous, harmful degrees. It's a fascinating dossier that dates back decades. It's a lengthy file, too, running to nearly 500 pages, and is comprised of a number of notable documents. But, here's the weird thing, the document contains a copy of the controversial Majestic 12 /Eisenhower Briefing Document on the Roswell UFO affair of

1947. Of interest, the copy of the EBD document in the Pandora file has a hand-written note on it stating that: "This cannot be authenticated as an official DoD document."

Logic suggests that the message was probably written around the end of 1988, which is when both the Air Force and the FBI were busily adding near-identical messages to their copies of the Majestic 12 documents. Exopaedia notes of the Pandora program that, in the early 1960s, "...the CIA discovered that the U.S. embassy in Moscow was 'bombarded' with EMR (electromagnetic radiation). The signal was composed of several frequencies. The Pandora Project was intended to investigate and gather data on this Russian experiment. The embassy personnel were not informed of the existence of the beam, nor of the Pandora project."

Exopaedia continues that, "the signal was intended to produce blurred vision and loss of mental concentration. Investigation on the effects on the embassy personnel, however, showed that they developed blood composition anomalies and unusual chromosome counts. Some people even developed a leukemia-like blood disease."

So, what we have here is a file on a program that dates back to the early 1960s and which was focused on major U.S. government concerns that the Soviets were up to no good – as was clearly the case. But, even so, that still does not provide the answer to an important question. Why is a very controversial and questionable document on dead aliens and crashed UFOs contained in a Department of Defense file on an old, Cold War-era operation instigated by the Russians? Attempts on my part – between 2014 and 2018 - to use the Freedom of Information Act to get the answers have failed to reveal anything of note. In fact, *of anything in the slightest.*

Game over? Not a chance. The shenanigans – and the issues concerning Russia and the Majestic 12 documents - continue. As you will now see.

15.

"SOME FORM OF TOXIN OR A HIGHLY CONTAGIOUS DISEASE"

As we saw in the previous chapter, there is strong available evidence that suggests the Russians were behind the notorious Majestic 12 documents, which publicly surfaced in 1987; even though Bill Moore and Jaime Shandera had copies in their hands since Christmas 1984. At the same time ufologists were salivating over the Majestic 12 papers in the eighties, the Russians were working to convince Americans that the U.S. government had secretly created AIDS, the Human Immunodeficiency Virus, or HIV. The purpose? To use the virus as the definitive doomsday weapon. It was nothing but tacky Russian propaganda. It's a strange and controversy-filled story that, in a very odd way, has a link to a *second* set of Majestic 12 documents; the new ones surfaced in the 1990s. This second set would provoke even more controversy than the original ones ever could. Before we get back to Majestic 12, though, let's take a look at the claims and rumors that the U.S. Government created HIV and how the whole situation played out. We have to turn our attentions to a U.S. Department of State document titled *AIDS as a Biological Weapon*, which I obtained thanks to the Freedom of Information Act. I'll present it to you without interruption:

When the AIDS disease was first recognized in the early 1980s, its origins were a mystery. A deadly new disease had suddenly appeared, with no obvious explanation of what had caused it. In such a situation, false rumors and misinformation naturally arose, and Soviet disinformation specialists exploited this situation as well as the musings of conspiracy theorists to help shape their brief but highly effective disinformation campaign on this issue. In March 1992, then-Russian intelligence chief and later Russian Prime Minister Yevgeny Primakov admitted that the disinformation service of the Soviet KGB had concocted the false story that the AIDS virus had been created in a U.S. military laboratory as a biological weapon. The Russian newspaper Izvestiya reported on March 19, 1992: "[Primakov] mentioned the well-known articles printed a few years ago in our central newspapers about AIDS supposedly originating from secret Pentagon laboratories." According to Yevgeny Primakov, the articles exposing U.S. scientists' "crafty" plots were fabricated in KGB offices. The Soviets eventually abandoned the AIDS disinformation campaign in their media under pressure from the U.S. government in August 1987.

In addition to the Soviet disinformation specialists, a tiny handful of fringe-group conspiracy theorists also espoused the false charge that the AIDS virus had been created as a biological weapon. One of them was Mr. Theodore Strecker, an attorney in the United States, who had a brother, Robert, who was a physician in Los Angeles. Theodore wrote a manifesto, "This is a Bio-Attack Alert" on March 28, 1986. He imagined that traitorous American doctors, United Nations bureaucrats, and Soviet officials were involved in a gigantic conspiracy to destroy the

United States with biological warfare. He wrote, "We have allowed the United Nations World Health Organization to combine with traitors in the United States National Institute of Health to start a Soviet Union attack." Mr. Strecker claimed that the "War on Cancer" led by the U.S. National Institutes of Health (NIH) was a cover for developing AIDS. He wrote, "the virologists of WHO [the World Health Organization], NCI [the U.S. National Institute of Cancer], and the NIH, have written in plain English their plan for conquest of America and are presently executing it disguised as cancer research. Mr. Strecker saw the Soviet Union at the heart of this alleged conspiracy: "This is an attempt to exhaust America with hatred, struggle, want, confusion, and inoculation of disease. The enemy intends to control our population with disease, make us dependent upon their remedies, engineer each birth, and reduce America to a servant of the Supreme Soviet."

Mr. Strecker sent his manifesto to the president and vice president of the United States, governors of several states, and various U.S. government departments, urging them to 'retake the virus labs using force if necessary' and other dramatic emergency measures. It did not have the galvanizing effect he had hoped. In the mid-1980s, there was still considerable confusion about how AIDS developed, although scientists universally agreed that it was a naturally occurring disease, not one that was man-made. In the intervening years, science has done much to solve this mystery. There is now strong scientific evidence that the AIDS virus originated as a subspecies of a virus that commonly infects the western equatorial African chimpanzee.

Today, among some of the most extreme conspiracy-theorists, the idea/rumor that AIDS was deliberately created as a biological weapon – possibly to lower population levels and to allow a global elite to take control of a smaller, decimated human race - still pervades. All of which brings us to the matter of a controversial batch of Majestic 12 papers that surfaced in the 1990s from a man named Timothy Cooper. Although no longer active in the UFO research community, Cooper, of Big Bear Lake, California, provoked a wealth of controversy for saucer-seekers when it was announced what he had in his possession. It was all "thanks" to an enormous body of allegedly leaked and highly secret documentation that had been given to Cooper under circumstances worthy of *All the President's Men*. Cooper was certainly no Woodward or Bernstein, but you get the point I'm making: Cooper had insider sources who were willing to significantly assist his UFO research by feeding him controversial papers on aliens and extraterrestrial spacecraft. Clandestine mail drops in the dead of night were very much the order of the day. The primary informants were an elderly man named "Thomas Cantwheel" and a woman named "Salina." The latter was said to have been Cantwheel's daughter. Both of them, Cooper was told, had worked in the field of U.S. counterintelligence for decades. They were the careful keepers of untold numbers of sinister secrets, some supposedly connected to the 1962 death of uber-babe, Marilyn Monroe, and to the November 22, 1963 assassination of President John F. Kennedy, in Dealey Plaza, Dallas, Texas. If you believe their words, that is.

It's important to note that if you do a Google search on "Cantwheel" you will find only links that deal with UFOs, Tim Cooper, and Majestic 12. The reason for this is very simple: "Cantwheel" is not a real name. Yet, that's the name Cooper's source consistently signed off on his communications to Cooper. The closest real name is "Cantwell." There's a reason for – and significance to – the oddness in relation to the names, as will become obvious when this chapter reaches its end.

Over a period of time that ran close to a decade, Cooper's informants provided him with what ultimately amounted to *thousands* of pages of saucer-themed material and additional data. They were focused on everything from the Majestic 12 committee and alien autopsies to accounts of crashed UFOs and attempts by the U.S. military to replicate extraterrestrial technology. One document even alluded to the possibility that the May 22, 1949, death of James Forrestal – the first U.S. Secretary of Defense – was not the suicide many assumed it was. Rather, the Cooper papers suggest, Forrestal had to be taken out of circulation to ensure that he didn't go public on what he knew about flying saucers. What really set the Cooper-era Majestic 12 documentation apart from that which caught the attention of the Moore-Shandera-Friedman team in the 1980s? It was references of deadly viruses; something that is the most significant part of the overall story, as you will now see.

In my 2017 book, *The Roswell UFO Conspiracy*, I wrote the following, which will demonstrate how I personally became so embroiled in the matter of the Cooper-era papers: "It's a little known fact that in late 2001, Tim Cooper sold all of his voluminous UFO files to Dr. Robert M. Wood. Bob is the author of *Alien Viruses* and the father of Ryan Wood, who has spent years researching alleged crashed UFO incidents – all detailed in his book, *Majic Eyes Only*. It is even less well-known that in the early days of 2002, Bob hired me to spend a week in an Orange County, California-based motel-room, surrounded by all of the thousands upon thousands of pages of Cooper's voluminous collection of the cosmic sort. The plan was for me to catalog all of the material, to compile each and every piece of it into chronological order, and to summarize the content of each document, every letter, and every Freedom of Information request that Cooper had submitted to government agencies – which is precisely what I did. It was a week in which I most definitely earned my loot. It was also a week that paralleled the infamous story told by Hunter S. Thompson in his classic gonzo saga, *Fear and Loathing in Las Vegas*. Whereas Thompson was hunkered down with his whisky, margaritas and shrimp cocktails, for me it was cases of cold beer and club sandwiches."

I could not fail to note just how much of the material that existed in Cooper's files was relative to stories of manufactured viruses, biological weaponry, and bizarre, medical conspiracies. Contained in Cooper's vast collection was a 1999 edition of Edward T. Haslam's book, *Mary, Ferrie & the Monkey Virus* ("Mary" being Mary Sherman, a cancer researcher who died under very strange, fiery circumstances in New Orleans in 1964, and "Ferrie" being David Ferrie, a man that New Orleans District Attorney Jim Garrison concluded was a conspirator in the death of JFK). Haslam's story is a controversial one. It mixes biological warfare and deadly viruses with a ruthless murder – and much more, too. And, as the back-cover of the book reveals, the story addresses "questions concerning the origins of the AIDS epidemic." In 2007, Haslam wrote *Dr. Mary's Monkey*, a lengthy book that added a wealth of new material to the Ferrie-Sherman-AIDS controversy.

Also contained in the Cooper files was a document titled *UFO Reports and Classified Projects*, in which I saw for the first time that aforementioned Orange County motel-room. It offers a very controversial, non-UFO-themed, explanation for what occurred at Roswell back in July 1947. I doubt that anyone in Ufology – aside from myself, Bob Wood and Tim Cooper – has ever seen the document in its original form. And I do mean "original." It's not a photocopy. The relevant extract reads as follows, in relation to 1947-era classified U.S. military programs:

> "One of the projects underway at that time incorporated re-entry vehicles containing radium and other radioactive materials combined with biological warfare agents developed by IG Farben for use against allied assault forces in Normandy in 1944. When a V-2 warhead impacted near the town of Corona, New Mexico, on July 4, 1947, the warhead did not explode and it and the deadly cargo lay exposed to the elements which forced the Armed Forces Special Weapons Project to close off the crash site and a cover story was immediately put out that what was discovered was the remains of a radar tracking target suspended by balloons."

Of IG Farben, the Holocaust Research Project states: "IG Farben was a German Limited Company that was a conglomerate of eight leading German chemical manufacturers, including Bayer, Hoechst and BASF, which at the time were the largest chemical firms in existence. Prior to the First World War these firms had established a community of interests – Interessengemeinschaft – hence the initials IG which merged into a single company on the 25 December 1925, thus constituting the largest chemical enterprise, in the whole world."

Britannica.com gets to the heart of the absolute worst part of IG Farben's "work." They note: "During World War II, IG Farben established a synthetic oil and rubber plant at Auschwitz in order to take advantage of slave labor; the company also conducted drug experiments on live inmates. After the war several company officials were convicted of war crimes (nine being found guilty of plunder and spoliation of property in occupied territory and four being found guilty of imposing slave labor and inhumane treatment on civilians and prisoners of war)."

Scum? Yep.

It appears – within the pages of the *UFO Reports and Classified Projects* document that Cooper acquired – that someone wanted to make a connection between the Roswell affair of 1947 and IG Farben. It's important to note, though, that Timothy Cooper specifically chose *not* to release this particular document into the public domain. In fact, it may well have been the *only* allegedly leaked document that he never made public. Why did Cooper choose to keep this report out of the hands of Ufology? I don't know. Perhaps it was too controversial for even Cooper, which is certainly saying something. What I can state for sure, however, is that had I not found the relevant papers in the voluminous files of Cooper back in 2002, it's highly doubtful that they would ever have surfaced. Most probably, had Cooper chosen to reveal the document, then it would have likely created a firestorm within Ufology. After all, linking the world's most famous UFO case with Holocaust-connected IG Farben would have provoked a huge controversy and created even more distrust about the actions of the U.S. Government. If the Soviets *were* behind the *UFO Reports and Classified Projects* document, then that may well have been the goal. But, that's not all.

Far more controversial is another supposedly leaked document titled *Majestic Twelve Project, 1ˢᵗ Annual Report*. Its subtitle makes the subject of the document clear: *A Review of the President's Special Panel to Investigate the Capture of Unidentified Planform Space Vehicles by U.S. Armed Forces and Agencies*. Oddly, the document lacks a date; however, it does not refer to any events or incidents that post-date 1951, which suggests it was written in that year. Or, written to make us *think* it was created in 1951. Cooper's notes

– the ones that I had access to in 2002 – show that he received the *Report* in three sections, rather than as one unified document. The cover-page turned up in Cooper's Big Bear Lake mailbox on January 19, 1994. It was almost a year later – specifically on December 30, 1994 – when Cooper obtained the Table of Contents. The rest of the document was provided to him on February 22, 1995.

It's important to note there are significant problems with the overall content of the *1ˢᵗ Annual Report*. By that, I mean it's a hoax; there is no doubt about it, whatsoever. I'll show you why: The membership of what is described as Majestic 12's "Special Panel" was said to have been the following: Dr. Vannevar Bush; General Hoyt S. Vandenberg, USAF; Brigadier General George [pF. Schulgen, USAF; Dr. J. Robert Oppenheimer; Detlev Bronk, of the National Research Council; Jerome Hunsaker, of the National Academy of Sciences; James Doolittle; Lieutenant General Lewis H. Brereton; Rear Admiral Paul F. Lee, Office of Naval Research; Major General George C. McDonald, USAF; Dr. Hugh L. Dryden; Admiral John Gingrich; Major General George C. McDonald, USAF; and Major General Luther D. Miller, U.S. Army.

In my summary report to Bob Wood, which was written shortly after I was finished with Cooper's voluminous files in Orange County, I stated the following: "General J. Lawton Collins is described as Deputy Chief of Staff, United States Army. In reality, Collins was Deputy Chief only from 1947 to mid-August 1949. He attained the rank of Chief of Staff on August 16, 1949 and held that position until August 15, 1953. Likewise, Major General Luther D. Miller is listed in the *Report* as Chief of Chaplains with the Army. He was, but only from 1945 to 1949. Similarly, the reference to Lieutenant General Lewis H. Brereton being Chairman of the Military Liaison Committee to the Atomic Energy Committee is incorrect: he was attached to the Liaison

Committee of the AEC in 1947 and through early 1948, but by June 1948 he was Secretary General of the Air Force. Hoyt S. Vandenberg is listed in the *Report* as Vice Chief of Staff with the U.S. Air Force; yet, in reality, he had attained the rank of Chief of Staff by April 30, 1948. George C. McDonald's name appears in the *Report* as the Director of Intelligence with the Air Force. McDonald was indeed appointed to that position – in October 1947. However, in June 1948, he became Chief of the Air Section of the United States' Military Commission at Rio de Janeiro, Brazil, and did not even return to the United States until June 1950, at which point he was assigned to the Office of the Department of the Deputy Chief of Staff for Personnel."

I continued to Bob Wood: "Quite clearly, there is a very recognizable trend here: whoever wrote the *1st Annual Report* specifically described the ranks held by the alleged members of the *Special Panel* in 1947 and into the early part of 1948 *only*. The ranks that practically *all* of the members held in 1947 and 1948 were utterly redundant by 1951." Someone screwed up.

For some Majestic 12 proponents, this was a big problem. For others, it wasn't: they just ignored this glaringly huge elephant in the room and stuck rigidly to their "I want to believe" stance. Then, there's the matter of a mysterious virus. The writer of the *1st Annual Report* went on to say:

BW [Biological Warfare] programs in U.S. and U.K. are in field test stages. Discovery of new virus and bacteria agents so lethal, that serums derived by genetic research, can launch medical science into unheard of fields of biology. The samples extracted from bodies found in New Mexico, have yielded new strains of a retro-virus not totally understood, but, give promise of the ultimate BW weapon. The danger lies in the spread of airborne and bloodborne outbreaks of diseases in large populations, with no medical cures available.

Current research in U.S. and U.K., can be accelerated when studies are complete. Understanding the human makeup through EBE ["Extraterrestrial Biological Entity," allegedly a term used by MJ12 to describe aliens] research will bring a varied wealth of information in how cells replicate themselves and may help in developing new drugs and markets. Healthcare industries are considered the best source of R&D for DoD programs.

In "Annex A" of the report there's this, which is equally controversial:

The Panel was concerned over the contamination of several SED personnel upon coming in contact with debris near the power plant. One technician was overcome and collapsed when he attempted the removal of a body. Another medical technician went into a coma four hours after placing a body in a rubber body-bag. All four were rushed to Los Alamos for observation. All four later died of seizures and profuse bleeding. All four were wearing protective suits when they came into contact with body fluids from the occupants. Autopsies on the four dead SED technicians are not conclusive. It is believed that the four may have suffered from some form of toxin or a highly contagious disease. Tissue samples are currently being kept at Fort Detrick, Md. In the opinion of the senior AEC medical officer, current medical equipment and supplies are wholly inadequate in dealing with a large scale outbreak of the alien virus.

In my report to Bob Wood, I added the following, which specifically addressed the references to Fort Detrick and the matter of retroviruses: "There are two aspects of these specific extracts [of the document] that have provoked extreme controversy within the tightly knit UFO research arena: namely, the allegation that tissue samples had been forwarded to Fort Detrick, and the reference to a poorly defined 'retrovirus.'"

I explained to Wood why, exactly, this was all very problematic: "*Medline*, the computerized database on biomedical research that has access to all medical related journals dating back to 1965, confirms that the first modern usage of the term retrovirus did not surface until the 1970s; and it was in the September 8, 1977 issue of *Nature* that we see the term first used in its now well-defined format. Similarly, the term retrovirus is actually derived from the first two letters of Reverse Transcriptase. Eleni Papadopolus-Eleopulos, a bio-physicist engaged in AIDS research states in her paper, *A brief history of Retroviruses*: 'Reverse transcriptase is an enzyme first discovered in Oncoviruses in 1970 hence their present name, retroviruses.' As Papadopolus-Eleopulos' statement makes clear, the term retrovirus was an outgrowth of terminology applied to an enzyme that was *not even discovered* until years after the *1ˢᵗ Annual Report* was allegedly written."

I also informed Bob Wood that, "…Fort Detrick did not receive that title until 1956: from 1943 until 1955 the installation was designated Camp Detrick, having previously been known as Detrick Field…This has led some commentators to suggest that, even though the *1ˢᵗ Annual Report* does not refer to *any* events that post-date 1951, the document *must*, therefore, be of 1956, or post-1956, vintage. This scenario, however, falls apart for one, specific reason. Of those listed as members of the Majestic 12 Special Panel, one is General Hoyt S. Vandenberg. Unfortunately, Vandenberg died in 1954. Therefore, he could not possibly have been a member of such a Panel in 1956, two years after his death."

Clearly, the *1st Annual Report* is not a genuine document; all of the available evidence is stacked solidly against it. But, we're not quite done. We now come to what may be the most important part of the whole story of Timothy Cooper and those so-called leaked documents. It's time to go back to the matter of the KGB and its 1980s-era plan to convince the world that certain elements of the U.S. Government engineered HIV for malicious purposes.

As the U.S. Department of State recorded: "In March 1992, then-Russian intelligence chief and later Russian Prime Minister Yevgeny Primakov admitted that the disinformation service of the Soviet KGB had concocted the false story that the AIDS virus had been created in a U.S. military laboratory as a biological weapon."

Now, let us take another look at certain, important threads contained in the *1st Annual Report*. The Majestic 12 papers reference a "new virus," "a retro-virus not totally understood," "blood-borne outbreaks of diseases," "the ultimate BW [Biological Warfare] weapon," "a highly contagious disease," and the connection between "Healthcare industries" and "DoD [Department of Defense] programs." Mirroring the above, it's a fact that HIV is a retrovirus. It's also a blood-borne virus. And, as the Department of State reported, the Russians were spreading a rumor that, "… the AIDS virus had been created in a U.S. military laboratory as a biological weapon." The additional rumor was that shadowy elements of the U.S. pharmaceutical industry were in on the conspiracy.

In light of all these distinct and undeniable parallels, it's very easy to see how some people – of an *extremely* conspiratorial mind – might come to believe that the discovery of such a dangerous alien virus, in 1947, and the recovery of a crashed UFO in New Mexico, led to the creation of HIV. It's a fact that of all the Majestic 12-themed papers that were provided to Cooper, it's this one – more than any other – which provoked so much controversy. Admittedly, the document is filled with suggestive threads that fit neatly within the parameters of the AIDS conspiracy theory. That may well have been the goal of the creators of the *1ˢᵗ Annual Report*.

Now, we come to the matter of that curious name of Timothy Cooper's primary informant, "Thomas Cantwheel." As I noted earlier in this chapter, "Cantwheel" is not a real name. And it never has been a real name, either. It is, however, very similar to a genuine one. That of "Cantwell." There may have been a very specific reason as to why "Cantwheel" chose that particular name when dealing with Cooper and with regards to a deadly virus with AIDS-like aspects attached to it. It might have been designed – as a less than subtle pointer - to have Cooper come to the conclusion that AIDS had been created by the U.S. Government, and that there was, incredibly, an extraterrestrial component to all of this. Check out the following from *Source Watch*:

> "Dr. Alan *Cantwell* [italics mine], author of *AIDS and the Doctors of Death: An Inquiry into the Origin of the AIDS Epidemic* and *Queer Blood: The Secret AIDS Genocide Plot*, believes that HIV is a genetically modified organism developed by U.S Government scientists; that it was introduced into the population through hepatitis B experiments performed on gay and bisexual men between 1978-1981 in Manhattan, Los Angeles, San Francisco, St. Louis, Denver, and Chicago (these experiments were directed by Dr. Wolf Szmuness); and that there is an ongoing government and media cover-up regarding the origin of the AIDS epidemic. Similar theories have been advanced

by Dr. Robert B. Strecker and by Milton William Cooper, author of *Behold a Pale Horse*."

Milton William Cooper, it should be noted, was one of the most controversial and over-the-top conspiracy-theorists of the 20th century. He died in a shoot-out, at his Eagar, Arizona home on November 5, 2001. Apache County sheriff's deputies were there to arrest him on an aggravated assault with a deadly weapon charge. Cooper was someone whose claims should be laid to rest, and particularly so the claim that AIDS was designed to deliberately target and kill people.

So, what do we have here? Well, we have tales of a highly dangerous retrovirus, of a Cantwell vs. a Cantwheel, of tainted blood, of big business in cahoots with the Pentagon, and of a mysterious couple of informants who were never really identified and who vanished into the ether (or who went back to Moscow…) after handing over controversial files to a UFO researcher who thought he was getting the real deal. Put all of that together and we have a heady brew of controversial proportions. Not only that, Dr. Alan Cantwell concluded that Fort Detrick played a role in all of this – a facility that appears in Timothy Cooper's Majestic 12 papers, too, in relation to research into a deadly alien virus, as you will recall.

Put all of these issues together and what do we have? I suggest that we have a very strange and highly alternative attempt, in the 1990s, to resurrect the Russians' "America created AIDS" disinformation program of the previous decade. But, this time (when *The X-Files* was extremely popular and the adventures of Mulder and Scully were reigniting U.S. public interest in UFOs) by carefully using crashed UFOs, dead aliens, and an extraterrestrial virus as the key components in the plot; all fabricated and completely bogus. Indeed, no-one should believe or conclude there is a real connection between HIV, AIDS and extraterrestrials. It's as ridiculous as it is offensive. For those who created the document, the problem was that Cooper chose to quit Ufology and sold all of his files to Bob Wood. And, when it came to the viral angle of all this, Cooper chose not to bite anyway. At least, as far as I could tell from his files, that is. Cooper may not even have appreciated the significance of the various, glaring threads, as well as that Cantwheel-Cantwell issue, strategically placed right in front of his eyes. Also, most of the UFO research community didn't buy into the Cooper material. Thus, the result was that the UFOs-Aliens-U.S. Government-AIDS operation stalled and finally died. Let's hope that it stays that way.

16.

"HOW COVERT AGENTS INFILTRATE THE INTERNET"

Now, in our final chapter, it's time to ask an important question: does this strange game of aliens, disinformation and lies still continue in today's world? Certainly, the vast majority of the programs designed to use the UFO subject as a tool of manipulation took place during the height of the Cold War; that much is abundantly clear. It should be noted, though, that while the available data is limited, we can say that UFOs – or, rather, the mystique and the legend that surrounds them – are still of interest to the intelligence services of several nations. In a strange way, the evidence has a link to the saga of none other than the ultimate 21st century whistleblower, Edward Snowden.

If, prior to 2013, someone were to ask you for your thoughts on Edward Snowden, you would almost certainly reply: "Who? Huh?" His family, friends, and work colleagues aside, Snowden was unknown. Just about completely. That all changed – and it changed radically – in the summer of 2013. That was when the shocking story of the National Security Agency's top secret programs of widespread surveillance came tumbling out into the public domain. It created shockwaves that are still reverberating to this day. Not only was Snowden suddenly the most talked about man on the planet, he was also – in many quarters – public enemy number one.

As Snowden revealed, and unbeknownst to just about everyone (the National Security Agency aside, of course), the NSA was spying not just on foreign nations but on U.S. citizens too – as in just about each and every one of them. Potentially, anyway. Landlines, cell-phones, email, Facebook, Twitter, and Skype: they had all been penetrated by the NSA, very often with the witting, subservient, and totally unforgivable, help of some of those same companies. The data collection process was so mind-bogglingly huge – maybe even wildly out of control - that it would likely have had even George Orwell himself shaking his head in disbelief; except for just one thing: Orwell's *1984* was fiction. This was all too real.

The responses to Snowden's revelations were interesting and thought-provoking. For some people, Snowden is the definitive American hero; someone who succeeded in demonstrating to the American people, and to the world at large, that the NSA was an agency run riot in its goal to place the entire United States under unending surveillance. For others, however, he is a man who has massively jeopardized U.S. national security, and placed our troops and agents in deep danger. There were even calls not for just his lifelong incarceration, but for his execution too, as the ultimate traitor. For many people, however, Snowden falls somewhere between both camps. And then there's the matter of UFOs. Or, at least, the lore surrounding it.

The story of Edward Snowden would never have soared to the levels that it did had it not been for the research of investigative journalist Glenn Greenwald. Having secured Snowden's trust, Greenwald was able to secure an astonishing amount of highly classified material on the NSA's surveillance programs. One of Snowden's lesser-known revelations revolved around a PowerPoint presentation produced by the U.K.'s Government Communications Headquarters, which is the nation's equivalent of its, ahem, big brother, the United States' NSA. The presentation was titled "How Covert Agents Infiltrate the Internet to Manipulate, Deceive and Destroy Reputations." Interestingly, the PowerPoint production – which, in part, provides ways and means to shatter the characters of people under surveillance - contained three photographs of alleged UFOs.

Mark Pilkington, a writer on, and an investigator of, the UFO subject has a particular interest in how government agencies have used the UFO controversy to their advantages. His 2010 book, *Mirage Men*, is subtitled: *An Adventure into Paranoia, Espionage, Psychological Warfare, and UFOs.* That will give you a very good idea as to where Pilkington is coming from in relation to UFOs. Journalist David Clarke asked Pilkington what he thought of all this. Pilkington said to Clarke: "We don't know why there are UFOs in this [PowerPoint] presentation. But the fact that the saucer photos appear within the context of influencing and manipulating online communities is highly suggestive."

As for Glenn Greenwald, he said of all this: "...these GCHQ documents are the first to prove that a major western government is using some of the most controversial techniques to disseminate deception online and harm the reputations of targets. Under the tactics they use, the state is deliberately spreading lies on the Internet about whichever individuals it targets, including the use of what GCHQ itself calls 'false flag operations' and emails to people's families and friends. Who would possibly trust a government to exercise these powers at all, let alone do so in secret, with virtually no oversight, and outside of any cognizable legal framework? Then there is the use of psychology and other social sciences to not only understand, but shape and control, how online activism and discourse unfolds."

And that's not the only example of UFO duplicity in the 21st century. It's time to return to the seemingly ever-present matter of Majestic 12. What you may have thought was over and done, was not quite so over and done, after all.

As I said in a June 16, 2017 article for the *Mysterious Universe* website titled *"The Majestic 12 Documents Are Back…,"* just like an over-the-hill, bloated rock band that doesn't know when it's time to retire and go away forever, the notorious saga of Majestic 12 hit the road and briefly toured again in 2017. Yes, those pesky documents were back once more. Or, rather, an entirely new and controversial set of papers were among us. Thoughts on the documentation was mixed: some researchers suggested the whole thing was someone's idea of a hoax. Others concluded that they were the real thing. Me? I went down the path marked "Disinformation." It's accurate to say that I still do. The new Majestic 12 files, which ran to 47-pages, were provided to Heather Wade. At the time, she was the host of the popular *Midnight in the Desert* show. I was on Heather's show several times and I like her. When she says that she got the documents from what was described as "a trusted source," I believe her. But, as time has shown, we never learned who Heather's source really was. And we were never told how that same source got the documents to her, or from where they came. There is no doubt, however, that these papers are *not* the real thing. Here's why:

First, there's the matter of the controversial, alleged UFO crash at Aztec, New Mexico in March 1948 – a case which we addressed early in the pages of this book, and in relation to conman Silas Newton, the Psychological Strategy Board, and CIA employee, Karl Pflock. The latest Majestic 12 documents contain a substantial amount of data on the alleged recovery at Hart Canyon, Aztec, of the UFO and its alien crew. But, here's the problem: the original Majestic 12 documents given to Jaime Shandera in 1984 and that surfaced in Timothy Good's book,

Above Top Secret specifically state that, after the Roswell affair of 1947, "a *second* object, probably of similar origin," came down in the "El Indio-Guerrero area area of the Texas-Mexico border" in December 1950. It's very important to note the December 1950 date and that word, "*second.*" And here's why it's so important:

The alleged 1952 Majestic 12 briefing for President-Elect Eisenhower states that Roswell was the first crash (in 1947), and that the Texas-Mexico event (in 1950) was the second one. Yet, in the new files we are told that Majestic 12 had recovered another UFO – the one reportedly found at Aztec, New Mexico in March 1948. We are now led to believe that Aztec was sandwiched between Roswell and El Indio-Guerrero. But, there's no mention of the Aztec incident in the documents published by Timothy Good, Bill Moore, Jaime Shandera and Stanton Friedman. Are/were the members of Majestic 12 such numbskulls that they couldn't even agree on how many UFOs came down, when they came down, and how many they had stored away? This was (so the unlikely tale goes) a briefing for the President-Elect! Telling Eisenhower about Roswell and El Indio-Guerrero, but avoiding mentioning Aztec, makes no sense at all. And if anyone tries to come up with a convoluted reason or justification as to why the Majestic 12 members would tell Eisenhower about Roswell but not about Aztec, don't even bother. You will just be digging a huge, steaming cesspit for yourself.

Still on the issue of Aztec, within the new material received by Heather Wade there is a bizarre transcript of what is alleged to be a series of chummy chats (I'm not exaggerating…) between "various interrogators" and an alien entity who, we learn, apparently survived the Aztec crash. At one point, the interviewer asks the "Extra-Terrestrial Biological Entity" the following question: "… so you have been visiting us for some time. I have no choice to accept that, even though I'd love some proof. But you still didn't tell me who sent you the message from Earth that brought you back?" [It's a long and tedious story…]

The alien replies to the interviewer: "Funny you should connect those two subjects." My response: WTF? Can you really imagine sitting opposite a creature from another world and which provides answers in what are so blatantly obviously human terms? On another occasion, the alien says, also in the kinds of words that we would use, "Listen now, because this could go on forever." And, at one point, the E.T. even refers to his great-grandfather. In those words! Are we *really* expected to believe this complete and utter crap? Well, someone might dearly have hoped such a thing would happen. Let's now take a look at some more of the problems with the papers provided to Heather Wade.

At one point in the documents, we're told that, regarding the Roswell affair, "…The authorities at the Roswell Field Army Air Forces Base were alerted by Mr. Brazel at 09:18 on 07 July, 1947 and two officers of the base were guided to the crash site by the ranch manager." *Wrong*. William Brazel, the ranch foreman who found the Roswell debris on the Foster Ranch back in 1947, did *not* contact the military at Roswell, at all. He contacted the local sheriff's office in Lincoln County and it was *they* who contacted the people at the Roswell base. Considering that this document was supposedly written by highly informed insiders, with access to the most detailed aspects of the Roswell event, you would think they would surely have gotten even the basic facts correct. But, seemingly not.

Roswell authority Kevin Randle revealed something important in relation to the security markings that can be found in the document: "The use of 'Ultra Top Secret' also raises questions. Ultra was the British code name for their operation to intercept and read high-level, highly-classified Nazi message traffic. This code name seems inappropriate for use by the U.S. government or military." "Inappropriate" is putting matters mildly; it's garbage.

Randle also noted: "We are treated to a reference to the base at Flat Rock, Nevada, which, of course, was the scene of much of the action in *The Andromeda Strain*." For those who may not know, *The Andromeda Strain* was a 1969 work of fiction from the late Michael Crichton. The movie version followed in 1971. There is no such real location as Flat Rock, Nevada. It was, and still is, the creation of Michael Chrichton and nothing else. Interestingly, *The Andromeda Strain* tells the story of an alien virus that wreaks havoc in an isolated area of the United States; a virus that has the potential to wipe out significant portions of the human race. This leads me to suspect that this latest document, and the 1990s-era Timothy Cooper material concerning a deadly alien virus, might very well have been written by the same person.

Now, we come to the theory that – just perhaps – the Russians were behind all of this. It's important to note that just because Heather Wade publicized the papers in 2017, it doesn't mean they were intended for use in a psy-op in that same year. After all, the document purports to be more than thirty years old. That being so, its pages may well have been originally planned for an operation back in the 1980s. Or, in the nineties. Are there any good reasons why the Russians may have been behind all of this? Let's see.

The highly talkative survivor from the Aztec crash of 1948 tells us a great deal about matters relative to aliens, to extraterrestrial technology, and to all kinds of matters of a UFO nature. But, the interviewee from the stars does something else, too: it proves to be quite critical of American politics and history. At one point, the military interviewer tells the alien sitting before him that "we [the human race] have changed," as a society, and that "Western civilization is now the leader in this world; for freedom and humanity."

The extraterrestrial, is far from being impressed by those words. It hits back hard and directly to the point: "...tell that to the millions of Hebrews your western civilization has destroyed in the past decade, or the millions of Negro families whose sons died to stop the madman Hitler, but who do not have plumbing in their homes."

It is a deeply unfortunate fact that blacks who fought in the Second World War *were*, in some cases, treated like second-class citizens. Writing at the *Smithsonian* website, Matthew Delmont says: "There is a historical relationship between Nazism and white supremacy in the United States. Yet the recent resurgence of explicit racism, including the attack in Charlottesville, has been greeted by many with surprise. But collective amnesia has consequences. When Americans celebrate the country's victory in WWII, but forget that the U.S. armed forces were segregated, that the Red Cross segregated blood donors or that many black WWII veterans returned to the country only to be denied jobs or housing, it becomes all the more difficult to talk honestly about racism today."

Military Times says: "…90 percent of black troops were forced to serve in labor and supply units, rather than the more prestigious combat units. Except for a few short weeks during the Battle of the Bulge in the winter of 1944 when commanders were desperate for manpower, all U.S. soldiers served in strictly segregated units."

The alien also castigates the United States' approach to Native Americans. It offers these words: "Not surprising, your history shows that the conqueror seldom preserves any history of their victims. I speak of the natives in this land mass; those called Indians; mostly on your eastern and southern borders and in the ribbon of land that connects yours to the southern continent. Navahos? Aztecs? Incas? The Olmec's and Toltec's cultures? These were all greater than your own civilization at a time when you were burning witches and killing their cats, which brought a plague that killed millions of your ancestors. Of course, you drove them mad and destroyed them with venereal diseases and smallpox; those you didn't slaughter for their gold."

Clearly, whoever put together this particular Majestic 12 document wished to make a point; a point that was focused on eras and situations destined, quite rightly and understandably, to provoke a high degree of shame when it comes to the United States. Moving on, the alien tells the interviewer that "...in a remote part of the nation you call Yugoslavia, we visited and helped the people there to build a very advanced culture over seven thousand years ago." Just muse upon that: of all the locations on the planet that the aliens could possibly have chosen to land and help humankind, they selected what became a significant communist land: Yugoslavia. The alien also goes on to say that back in 1895 creatures of its kind made contact with none other than a brilliant maverick scientist, Nikola Tesla.

It's a fact that Tesla – born in Croatia in 1856 and way ahead of his time - did indeed believe he was in contact with extraterrestrials. The *Richmond Times*, on January 13, 1901, stated: "There are thousands of people living in the world today who do not believe that the planet of Mars is inhabited. There are many others who do, and some of the leaders in science and foremost men in thought and invention are members of this last-named class. Nikola Tesla, the inventor of the wireless telegraphy, is one of these. Astronomers tell us that the planet Mars is several millions of years older than the earth and H. G. Wells, novelist, in one of his fantastic creations, has peopled this planet with a race of strange creatures. One thing, however, stands to reason, and that is this: If Mars is inhabited those inhabitants are far in advance of us as regards sciences, both theoretical and applied. This is what Tesla thinks, and why he is of the opinion has just recently been made known. He is convinced that the Martians are trying to communicate with us."

Similar accounts of Tesla's beliefs in alien contact proliferated in the media of the 20th century. They still do: on the History Channel's show, *Ancient Aliens*, if few places else. The alien in the Majestic 12 document advises the U.S. military that the United States had utterly failed to embrace the incredible technology which Tesla had perfected and that just might have enriched the world for each and every one of us. But, the creature was careful to add, the Soviets had, for a number of years, been running a "strong program of research" that was going ahead "inside the Soviet Union." In other words, the Russians were forging ahead, while we were fucking up.

Now, it's time to bring the Christian God into the equation.

In *The ABC of Communism*, N.I. Bukharin and E. Preobrazhensky, wrote: "'Religion is the opium of the people,' said Karl Marx. It is the task of the Communist Party to make this truth comprehensible to the widest possible circles of the laboring masses. It is the task of the party to impress firmly upon the minds of the workers, even upon the most backward, that religion has been in the past and still is today one of the most powerful means at the disposal of the oppressors for the maintenance of inequality, exploitation, and slavish obedience on the part of the toilers. Many weak-kneed communists reason as follows: 'Religion does not prevent my being a communist. I believe both in God and in communism. My faith in God does not hinder me from fighting for the cause of the proletarian revolution.' This train of thought is radically false. Religion and communism are incompatible, both theoretically and practically."

In light of this, it's worth noting that the alleged alien from the Aztec crash cautioned on relying on God in the years ahead of us. The creature explains that our civilization, which was first exposed to the alien race thousands of years ago, "did forget us."

That "your people seem to have undergone a period of history in which you were so afraid of old truths, that you erased them in favor of religious fantasy. Some of your people remembered us orally in their legends."

As the interview winds down to its end, the alien says that one day we will come to know its very own people in a fashion that will benefit one and all. Providing, that is, it doesn't come via "religious leaders."

The words of an alien or the carefully created statements of a Russian operative? I'll go with the latter.

Well into the 21st century, the meddling has clearly not gone away.

BIBLIOGRAPHY

"1977 Senate MKULTRA Hearing: Appendix A." http://www.druglibrary.org/schaffer/history/e1950/mkultra/AppendixA.htm. 2019.

"A Brief Chronicle of Retrovirology." https://www.ncbi.nlm.nih.gov/books/NBK19403/. 1997.

"Aetherius Society." Special Branch file, declassified under the terms of the U.K. Freedom of Information Act.

"The Aetherius Society." https://www.aetherius.org/. 2019.

"AIDS as a Biological Weapon." U.S. Department of State. 2005.

"AIDS conspiracy." https://www.sourcewatch.org/index.php/AIDS_conspiracy. January 24, 2006.

Albarelli, Jr., H.P. *A Terrible Mistake: The Murder of Frank Olson and the CIA's Secret Cold War Experiments.* Walterville, OR: Trine Day LLC, 2009.

Alliance for Human Research Protection. "1952: Stanley Glickman was another human casualty of Sydney Gottlieb's LSD antics." https://ahrporg/1952-stanley-glickman-was-another-human-casualty-of-sidney-gottliebs-lsd-antics/. 2019.

"Andrei Sakharov." https://www.nobelprize.org/prizes/peace/1975/sakharov/biographical/. 2019.

Angelucci, Orfeo. *Son of the Sun*. Los Angeles, CA: DeVorss & Co., 1959.

Angelucci, Orfeo. *The Secret of the Saucers*. Amherst, WI: Amherst Press, 1955.

Atomic Heritage Foundation. "Lavrentiy P. Beria." https://www.atomicheritage.org/profile/lavrentiy-p-beria. 2019.

Bailey, Martin. "Close encounters of an alien kind - and now if you've read enough about the election, here's news from another world." *Observer*, May 31, 1987.

BBC. "1960s: Thousands protest against H-bomb." http://news.bbc.co.uk/onthisday/hi/dates/stories/april/18/newsid_2909000/2909881.stm. 2018.

Bennett, Colin. *Looking for Orthon: The story of George Adamski, the first flying saucer contactee, and how he changed the world*. NY: Paraview Press, 2001.

Berlitz, Charles & Moore, William. *The Roswell Incident*. St. Albans, U.K.: Granada Publishing Limited, 1981.

Bethurum, Truman. *Aboard a Flying Saucer*. Los Angeles, CA: DeVorss & Co., Publishers, 1954.

Bishop, Greg. *Project Beta: The Story of Paul Bennewitz, National Security, and the Creation of a Modern UFO Myth*. NY: Paraview Pocket Books, 2005.

Blomqvist, Hakan. "The Enigma of Sonja Lyubicin." https://ufoarchives.blogspot.com/2018/04/the-enigma-of-sonja-lyubicin.html. April 26, 2018.

Blum, Howard. *Out There: The Government's Secret Quest for Extraterrestrials*. NY: Simon & Schuster, 1990.

Bragalia, Anthony. "Area 51 Book Exposed: Source for Roswell Story Named and Interviewed!" https://www.ufoexplorations.com/area-51-book-exposed-source-for-ros. May 2011.

Brewer, Jack. "Crashed Saucer Misinformation." https://ufotrail.blogspot.com/2017/07/crashed-saucer-misinformation.html. July 11, 2017.

Bukharin, N.I. & Preobrazhensky, E. "The ABC of Communism." https://www.marxists.org/archive/bukharin/works/1920/abc/11.htm. 2019.

"Campaign for Nuclear Disarmament." https://ipfs.io/ipfs/QmXoypizjW3WknFiJnKLwHCnL72vedxjQkDDP1mXWo6uco/wiki/Campaign_for_Nuclear_Disarmament.html. 2019.

Central Intelligence Agency. "The Bay of Pigs Invasion." https://www.cia.gov/news-information/featured-story-archive/2016-featured-story-archive/the-bay-of-pigs-invasion.html. 2019.

Clarke, David. *How UFOs Conquered the World: The History of a Modern Myth*. London, U.K.: Aurum Press, Ltd., 2015.

Clarke, David & Roberts, Andy. *Flying Saucerers: A Social History of UFOlogy*. Loughborough, U.K.: Alternative Albion, 2007.

"Communism." https://rationalwiki. org/wiki/Communism. 2019.

Coppens, Philip. "M-J12: Majestic, or Incredulous?" https://www.eyeofthepsychic.com/majestic12/. 2019.

Corbyn, Jeremy. "Labour figures slam claim that Michael Foot was paid by Soviets." https://www.theguardian.com/ politics/2018/sep/15/labour-figures-slam-claim-that-michael-foot-was-paid-by-soviets. September 15, 2018.

Cornwell, Rupert. "Obituary: Sydney Gottlieb." https:// www.independent.co.uk/arts-entertainment/obituary-sidney-gottlieb-1080920.html. March 16, 1999.

Corrales, Scott. "The UMMO Experience: Are You Experienced?" http://www.strangemag.com/ummo.html. 2019.

Corydon, Bent & Hubbard, Jr., L. Ron. *L. Ron Hubbard: Messiah or Madman?* Secaucus, NJ:Lyle Stuart Inc., 1987.

"Counterintelligence." https://www.fbi.gov/ investigate/counterintelligence. 2019.

Cruickshank, Douglas. "The CIA's purple haze." https:// www.salon.com/1999/05/06/cia/. May 6, 1999.

Currey, Cecil B. *Edward Lansdale: The Unquiet American*. Boston, MA: Houghton Mifflin, 1998.

Delmont, Matthew. "Why African-American Soldiers Saw World War II as a Two-Front Battle." https://www.smithsonianmag.com/history/why-african-american-soldiers-saw-world-war-ii-two-front-battle-180964616/. August 24, 2017.

Diamond, Jeremy. "Trump sides with Putin over US intelligence." https://www.cnn.com/2018/07/16/politics/donald-trump-putin-helsinki-summit/index.html. July16, 2018.

Empire News. "Flying Saucer Clubs Probe: Peace Messages 'from outer space.'" May 26, 1957.

"The establishment of ASIO." https://www.asio.gov.au/about/history/establishment-asio.html. 2018.

Fantastic Fiction. "Bernard Newman." https://www.fantasticfiction.com/n/bernard-newman/2019.

Feschino, Frank. *The Braxton County Monster: The Cover-Up of the Flatwoods Monster Revealed.* Charleston, WV: Quarrier Press, 2004.

"The Flying Wing." http://www.roswellfiles.com/FOIA/FlyingWing.htm. 2019.

Gaia Staff. "Project Serpo and the Zeta Reticuli Exchange Program." April 26, 2017.

General Accounting Office. *Results of a Search for Records Concerning the 1947 Crash Near*

Roswell, New Mexico. Washington, D.C.: U.S. Government Printing Office, July 28, 1995.

"George Adamski." Federal Bureau of Investigation file, declassified under the terms of the U.S. Freedom of Information Act.

Goff, Kenneth. *Red Shadows*. Englewood, CO: Self-published, 1959.

Good, Timothy. *Above Top Secret: The Worldwide UFO Cover-Up*. NY: William Morrow, 1988.

Goodman, David. "Radio's Civic Ambition: American Broadcasting and Democracy in the 1930s." http://www.oxfordscholarship.com/view/10.1093/acprof:oso/9780195394085.001.0001/acprof-9780195394085-chapter-6. 2011.

Gorightly, Adam & Bishop, Greg. *"A" is for Adamski*. CA: Gorightly Press, 2018.

Graham, Robbie. *Silver Screen Saucers: Sorting Fact from Fantasy in Hollywood's UFO Movies*. Hove, U.K.: White Crow Books, 2015.

Greenewald, John. "New Majestic-12 (MJ-12) Briefing Documents Released June 2017." https://www.the-blackvault.com/casefiles/new-majestic-12-mj-12-briefing-documents-released-june-2017/. June 13, 2017.

Greenwald, Glenn. "How Covert Agents Infiltrate the Internet to Manipulate, Deceive, and Destroy

Reputations." https://theintercept.com/2014/02/24/
jtrig-manipulation/. February 24, 2014.

Haines, Gerald K. "CIA's Role in the Study of
UFOs, 1947-90." https://www.cia.gov/library/
center-for-the-study-of-intelligence/csi-publications/
csi-studies/studies/97unclass/ufo.html. 1997.

Harry S. Truman Presidential Library & Museum. ", Staff
Member and Office Files: Psychological Strategy Board Files."
https://www.trumanlibrary.org/hstpaper/physc.htm. 2019.

Harvey, Peter & Keatley, Patrick. "From the archive, 25
September 1971: Britain expels 90 diplomat spies." https://
www.theguardian.com/world/2014/sep/25/britain-rus-
sia-spies-expelled-archive-1971. September 25, 2014.

Haslam, Edward T. *Dr. Mary's Monkey: How the unsolved murder
of a doctor, a secret laboratory in New Orleans and cancer-causing monkey viruses are linked to Lee Harvey Oswald, the JFK assassination
and emerging global epidemics.* Walterville, OR: TrineDay, 2015.

Haslam, Edward T. *Mary, Ferrie & the Monkey Virus: The
Story of an Underground Medical Laboratory.* Bradenton,
FL: Wordsworth Communications, 1999.

Heiser, Michael. "Project Pandora and the MJ-12 Eisenhower
Briefing Document." http://drmsh.com/project-pando-
ra-and-the-mj-12-eisenhower-briefing-document/July 18, 2014.

Heretic Among Heretics. "Jacques Vallee Interview." http://
www.ufoevidence.org/documents/doc839.htm. 2019.

Hohn, Maria. "African-American GIs of WWII: Fighting for democracy abroad and at home." https://www.militarytimes.com/military-honor/black-military-history/2018/01/30/african-american-gis-of-wwii-fighting-for-democracy-abroad-and-at-home/January 30, 2018,

Holocaust Encyclopedia. "Josef Mengele." https://encyclopedia.ushmm.org/content/en/article/josef-mengele. 2019.

Hungerford, Jean M. "The Exploitation of Superstitions for Purposes of Psychological Warfare." https://www.rand.org/content/dam/rand/pubs/research_memoranda/2008/RM365.pdf. April 14, 1950.

"IG Farben." https://www.britannica.com/topic/IG-Farben. 2019.

"In Honor of Jim Moseley." https://www.jimmoseley.com/ 2019.

Introvigne, Massimo. "L. Ron Hubbard, Kenneth Goff, and the 'Brain-Washing Manual' of 1955." https://www.cesnur.org/2005/brainwash_13.htm. 2019.

Jacobsen, Annie. *Area 51: An Uncensored History of America's Top Secret Military Base*. NY: Little, Brown and Company, 2011.

John F. Kennedy Presidential Library and Museum. "The Bay of Pigs." https://www.jfklibrary.org/learn/about-jfk/jfk-in-history/the-bay-of-pigs. 2019.

"Joseph McCarthy." https://www.history.com/top-ics/cold-war/joseph-mccarthy. April 15, 2019.

Keith, Jim. *Casebook on the Men in Black.*
Lilburn, GA: IllumiNet Press, 1997.

"Kenneth Arnold." http://www.pro-ject1947.com/fig/ka.htm. 2019.

"Kenneth Goff." Federal Bureau of Investigation file, declassi-fied under the terms of the U.S. Freedom of Information Act.

"Kenneth Goff." https://en.wikipedia.org/wiki/Kenneth_Goff. 2019.

"KGB." https://www.history.com/top-ics/russia/kgb. August 21, 2018.

Korkis, Jim. "Ward Kimball and UFOs." https://mouse-planet.com/9720/Ward_Kimball_and_UFOs. 2019.

Lamiroy, Manuel. "Pandora Project." http://www.exopaedia.org/Pandora+Project. 2019.

Leslie, Desmond & Adamski, George. *Flying Saucers Have Landed.* London, U.K.: Werner Laurie, 1953.

Letter of October 24, 2017 from the Federal Bureau of Investigation to John Greenewald. Reproduced at this link: http://documents.theblackvault.com/documents/fbifiles/paranormal/orfeoangelucci-fbi1.pdf. 2017.

Lewis, Paul. "Harry Rositzke, 91, linguist and American Spymaster." https://www.nytimes.com/2002/11/08/us/harry-rositzke-91-linguist-and-american-spymaster.html. November 8, 2002.

Los Angeles Times. "Shamanistic Order to be Established Here." April 1934.

Magic Tricks. "The War Magician." https://www.magictricks.com/war-magician.html. 2019.

"Majestic 12." Federal Bureau of Investigation file, declassified under the terms of the U.S.

Freedom of Information Act. https://vault.fbi.gov/Majestic%2012.. 2019.

"Marshal Tito Biography." https://www.notablebiographies.com/St-Tr/Tito-Marshal.html. 2019.

"Marshal Tito Facts." https://biography.yourdictionary.com/marshal-tito. 2019.

Maskelyne, Jasper. *Magic: Top Secret*. London, U.K.: S. Paul Publishers, 1949.

Merlan, Anna. "In 1951, the FBI Thought the Soviets Might be Hiding an Atomic Bomb

Somewhere in New York City." https://www.villagevoice.com/2014/07/22/

in-1951-the-fbi-thought-the-soviets-might-be-hiding-an-atomic-bomb-somewhere-in-new-york-city/. July 22, 2014.

Moore, William L. & Shandera, Jaime H. *The MJ-12 Documents: An Analytical Report.* Burbank, CA: The Fair Witness Project, 1990.

Moseley, James. *Saucer News*, June-July, 1955.

Moseley, James W. & Pflock, Karl T. *Shockingly Close to the Truth!* NY: Prometheus Books, 2002.

National Investigations Committee on Aerial Phenomena. "Project Grudge." http://www.nicap.org/grudge/grudge_dir.htm. 2019.

New York Times. "Frank Scully, Columnist, Dies; Defied Disabilities With Jests; Author of Several Books; Spent Much of His Life as Hospital Patient." https://www.nytimes.com/1964/06/25/archives/rank-scully-columnist-dies-defied-disabilities-with-jests-author-of.html. June 25, 1964.

Newman, Bernard. *The Flying Saucer.* Yardley, PA: Westholme Publishing, LLC, 2010.

"Nikola Tesla Promises Communication With Mars." *Richmond Times*, January 13, 1901.

"Oleg Gordievsky." https://en.wikipedia.org/wiki/Oleg_Gordievsky. 2019.

Pflock, Karl T. "What's Really Behind the Flying Saucers? A New Twist on Aztec." *The Anomalist, No. 8*. San Antonio, TX: *The Anomalist*, 2000.

Phillips, Julie. *James Tiptree, Jr.: The Double Life of Alice B. Sheldon*. NY: Picador, 2007.

Pilkington, Mark. *Mirage Men: An Adventure into Paranoia, Espionage, Psychological Warfare, and UFOs*. NY: Skyhorse Publishing, 2010.

Ramsey, Scott. *The Aztec UFO Incident: The Case, Evidence, and Elaborate Cover-up of One of the Most Perplexing Crashes in History*. Wayne, NJ: New Page Books, 2016.

Randle, Kevin D. "MJ-12 - New Documents, Old Story." http://kevinrandle.blogspot.com/2017/06/mj-12-new-documents-old-story.html. June 15, 2017.

Redfern, Nick. Interview with Colin Bennett, July 19, 2009.

Redfern, Nick. Interview with Jim Moseley, July 15, 2009.

Redfern, Nick. "MJ12: The FBI Connection." Self-published, 1996.

Redfern, Nick. "More on 'Mind Control,' UFOs & Conspiracy." https://mysteriousuniverse.org/2017/07/more-on-mind-control-ufos-conspiracy/. July 12, 2017.

Redfern, Nick. "The Majestic 12 Documents Are Back." https://mysteriousuniverse.org/2017/06/the-majestic-12-documents-are-back/. June 16, 2017.

Redfern, Nick. *The NASA Conspiracies. The Truth Behind the Moon Landings, Censored Photos, and the Face on Mars.* Wayne, NJ: New Page Books, 2010.

Redfern, Nick. *The Roswell UFO Conspiracy: Exposing a Shocking and Sinister Secret.* Bracey, VA: Lisa Hagan Books, 2017.

"Robertson Panel." http://www.cufon.org/cufon/robert.htm. 2019.

Sanderson, David. "MI6 believed Michael Foot was a paid Soviet Informant." https://www.thetimes.co.uk/article/mi6-believed-michael-foot-was-paid-soviet-informant-vpdtg3lgx. September 15, 2018.

Scully, Frank. *Behind the Flying Saucers.* NY: Henry Holt and Company, 1950.

"The Secret KGB UFO Files." https://www.imdb.com/title/tt0224072/. 1998.

"The Secret KGB UFO Files: The Russian Crash of 1969."https://www.ufocasebook.com/russia1969.html." 2019.

Senate Select Committee on Intelligence Activities. *Alleged Assassination Plots Involving Foreign Leaders: Interim Report of the Select Committee to Study Governmental*

Operations with Respect to Intelligence Activities. Washington, D.C.: U.S. Government Printing Office 1975.

"Senator Joseph McCarthy, McCarthyism, and the Witch Hunt." http://www.coldwar.org/articles/50s/senatorjosephmccarthy.asp. 2019.

Stringfield, Leonard H. *Situation Red: The UFO Siege*. London, U.K.: Sphere Books Limited, 1978.

Taylor, Philip. "The Mystic and the Spy: Two Early British UFO Writers." http://magonia.haaan.com/1997/the-mystic-and-the-spy-two-early-british-ufo-writers/. January 11, 1997.

"Thomas A. Parrott." http://www.arlington-cemetery.net/taparrott.htm. July 15, 2007.

Tristan. "The Two Men Who Went Missing Looking for a UFO." https://bizarreandgrotesque.com/2015/07/19/the-two-men-who-went-missing-looking-for-a-ufo/. July 19, 2015.

"Truman Bethurum." Federal Bureau of Investigation file, declassified under the terms of theU.S. Freedom of Information Act.

"UFO." Federal Bureau of Investigation file, declassified under the terms of the U.S. Freedom of Information Act. https://vault.fbi.gov/UFO. 2019.

UFO files declassified under the terms of the Australian Freedom of Information Act.

UFO files declassified under the terms of the U.S. Freedom of Information Act by the Defense Intelligence Agency.

UFO files declassified under the terms of the U.S. Freedom of Information Act by the National Security Agency.

"UFORQ Legends." http://uforq.asn.au/ufo-rq-legends/. 2019.

United States Air Force. Press Conference, the Pentagon, Washington, D.C., July 4, 1997.

United States Air Force. *The Roswell Report: Case Closed.* Washington D.C.: U.S. Government Printing Office, 1997.

United States Air Force. *The Roswell Report: Fact vs. Fiction in the New Mexico Desert.* Washington, D.C.: U.S. Government Printing Office, 1995.

United States Senate. "Joseph R. McCarthy." https://www.senate.gov/artandhistory/history/common/generic/Featured_Bio_McCarthy.htm. 2019.

Vallee, Jacques. *Messengers of Deception: UFO Contacts and Cults.* Berkeley, CA: And/Or Press. 1979.

Vallee, Jacques. *Revelations: Alien Contact and Human Deception.* NY: Ballantine, 1991.

Vankin, Jonathan & Whalen, John. *The 80 Greatest Conspiracies of all Time.* NY: Citadel, 2004.

"VOKS." http://documentstalk.com/wp/voks/. 2008.

'Ward Kimball." https://en.wikipedia.
org/wiki/Ward_Kimball. 2019.

Webb, Chris. Holocaust Research Project. "I.G.
Farben." http://www.holocaustresearchpro-
ject.org/economics/igfarben.html. 2010.

Wilkinson, Stephan. "The Horten Brothers' Jet
Flying Wing." https://www.historynet.com/hort-
en-brothers-jet-flying-wing.htm. January 30, 2019.

Wood, Dr. Robert M. & Wood, Ryan. *The Majestic Documents*.
Redwood City, CA: Wood & Wood Enterprises, 1998.

Wood, Ryan S. *Majic Eyes Only: Earth's Encounters
with Extraterrestrial Technology*. Broomfield,
CO: Wood Enterprises, 2005.

ACKNOWLEDGMENTS

I would like to offer my sincere thanks to my agent, friend and publisher, Lisa Hagan; my editor and co-publisher, Beth Wareham; book-designer, Simon Hartshorne; and Denise Rector, for the kind use of her "Flatwoods Monster"-themed photograph.

ABOUT THE AUTHOR

Nick Redfern is the author of more than 50 books on UFOs, the Loch Ness Monster, Bigfoot, zombies, and Hollywood scandal. His books include *The Roswell UFO Conspiracy*; *Women in Black*; *Men in Black*; *Nessie*; *Chupacabra Road Trip*; *The Black Diary*; and *365 Days of UFOs*. He is a regular on the Travel Channel's show, *In Search of Monsters*. Nick has also appeared on the BBC's *Out of This World*; the SyFy Channel's *Proof Positive*; the History Channel's *Monster Quest*, and *America's Book of Secrets;* the National Geographic Channel's *Paranatural;* and MSNBC's *Countdown* with Keith Olbermann. Nick lives in Arlington, Texas.

He can be contacted at his blog: http://nickredfernfortean.blogspot.com